LEAKING:

Who Does It?
Who Benefits?
At What Cost?

A Twentieth Century Fund Paper

LEAKING:

Who Does It?
Who Benefits?
At What Cost?

BY ELIE ABEL

Priority Press Publications/New York/1987

The Twentieth Century Fund is a research foundation undertaking timely analyses of economic, political, and social issues. Not-for-profit and non-partisan, the Fund was founded in 1919 and endowed by Edward A. Filene.

Library of Congress Cataloging-in-Publication Data
Abel, Elie.
  Leaking: who does it? who benefits? at what cost?

  "A Twentieth Century Fund paper"
  Bibliography: p.
  Includes index.
  1. Official secrets—United States. 2. Government information—United States. 3. Mass media—United States. 4. Press—United States. I. Title.
JK468.S4A63 1987 / 353.0071'45   87-25762
ISBN: 0-87078-218-5

Foreword

The press has often been called the handmaiden of government. Certainly that was the case when journalists who covered government operations, whether at the federal, state, or local level, dutifully reported what they received by way of news releases or statements from government officials. Today, the press is much less likely to rely solely on government spokesmen. To the contrary, stories frequently cite the reaction of the political opposition or of so-called objective analysts from the academic community. Yet in one sense, the press today is even more a handmaiden of its news sources than ever before. With the growth of government, we have seen a growth of news leakers, those government officials who, for one reason or another, provide reporters with unofficial and anonymous information about the activities of government.

For the most part, such leaks are useful. They add a great deal to the public's understanding of government. They also tend to make government more accountable than it otherwise would be. This is not to deny that leaks sometimes lead to abuse. Some information, not much fortunately, might better be kept secret. Other information is made available in distorted or exaggerated form, which can result in mistaken policies. The press, of course, does not much care about the motives of its sources. If something is news, it wants to get a beat on its competition, going on the air or rushing into print with what it has learned. There have always been leakers, and with a free press, there always will—and should—be, yet we ought to recognize that when the reporter acts as the handmaiden of the leaker without revealing the probable self-interest of his informant, something of an ethical conspiracy takes place.

The Twentieth Century Fund has long been interested in the problems and practices of the media. Thus, when Elie Abel suggested doing a paper on leaks, we were delighted to provide support for it. Abel, a veteran journalist with experience in both newspapers and television, served as dean of Columbia's Graduate School of Journalism before taking his present position as Harry and Norman Chandler Professor of Communication at Stanford. He is as well placed as any journalist-scholar to take on this complicated and intriguing assignment. In the paper that follows, he provides some historical background on leaks, and discusses why and how they take place.

He goes on to consider what, if anything, can be done about leaks and leakers. It is his view that nothing can or should be done to muzzle leakers but that the press might consider taking voluntary action to be somewhat more responsible in making clear the motives of those who leak. His paper is, I think, useful and informative and wise on leaking, recognizing both the value and the limitations of leaks. We at the Fund are grateful to him for it.

M. J. Rossant, DIRECTOR
The Twentieth Century Fund
September 1987

Contents

1 / How the Game Is Played in Washington

The relationship between sources and journalists resembles a dance, for sources seek access to journalists and journalists seek access to sources. Although it takes two to tango . . . more often than not, sources do the leading.

—*Herbert J. Gans, in* Deciding What's News

Americans are increasingly uneasy about the power of their government—its size, its cost, its many failures at problem solving. They are only slightly less uneasy about the press. Poll after poll ranks Congress and the federal bureaucracy a notch or two below the press at the low end of the confidence scale. The press is widely faulted for its frequent sloppiness with facts, its taste for cheap sensation, its claims to know more than in fact it does, and its free-and-easy attitude toward publication of government secrets that may conceivably harm the national interest.

There is, of course, nothing inherently disreputable about reporters seeking access to news sources. That is what they are paid for and expected to do. As for the sources at every level of government, from Deaf Smith County, Texas, to Washington, D.C., they need access to reporters in order to reach the broad public with information the administration of the day wants disseminated. If the sources do the leading much of the time, as Professor Gans suggests, that is a natural consequence of the fact that the dancers are not equal partners. The federal government is, among other things, a vast repository of information about the state of the nation and the world, gathered and assembled at the taxpayers' expense. News organizations, even the biggest of them, possess few such resources of their own. The source-reporter relationship, uncomfortable at times, but inescapable, is essential to an informed public opinion.

1

The Iran-contra affair is an excellent example of the dance between press and government. Even though there is no love lost between the partners in the dance, they remain locked in close embrace. On the other hand, it was not prying reporters but Attorney General Edwin Meese who made the original disclosure that the United States had sold arms to Iran, in direct contradiction of long-proclaimed national policy, and diverted part of the profits to support of the contra forces in Nicaragua. Once that secret was out, the press mobilized its investigative reporters to fill the gaps in the official story. Soon one disclosure followed another, some authorized, many not, mostly attributed to unnamed sources. Washington has seldom witnessed such an outpouring of anonymous information. Two words were on everyone's lips—"leak" and "plant."

President Reagan's early reaction was to denounce the press as a school of sharks drawn by blood in the water. The remarkable fact about the Iran-contra affair, however, was that the secret transactions *remained* secret for some fifteen months—from August 1985, when the first shipment was delivered, to November 1986, when the attorney general announced his preliminary finding.

The frenzy of fact seeking that followed involved, in addition to the press, four congressional committees and an independent counsel—and led to a drastic shake-up in the White House staff, including the National Security Council.

The dance between sources and journalists has a vocabulary of its own. The true leak is an unsolicited act by a source, in all but a handful of cases a *government* source, who makes sensitive information available to a reporter on condition that the leaker's identity shall not be disclosed. It is seldom the product of a reporter's probing. More typically, it is a premeditated act on the part of the leaker. Some leaks are authorized by higher authority. Others are clandestine. Purists in the Washington press corps insist that an authorized leak is better described as a *plant*, a disclosure designed to advance administration interests and goals.

Leaks proliferate in times of controversy and crisis. Although they spring from a variety of motives, to be examined in subsequent chapters, they have one common purpose: to serve the vested interest of the source. While the reporter also benefits by coming away with a story ahead of his competitors, the source has an additional advantage. If pressed after publication, he can safely deny or disavow on the record the very information he surreptitiously supplied to the reporter. Anonymity is his shield.

One Version of the Dance

I saw this process of self-protection at work more than thirty years ago as a young reporter for *The New York Times*, assigned to the Pentagon. My source was an army general. The story he told me in elaborate detail one afternoon, in the presence of about a dozen staff officers gathered around his conference table, had to do with plans for reshaping the traditional structure of the army division to meet the conditions of the new nuclear age. The general was proud of his handiwork. He could not have been more accommodating. My account of that briefing appeared the following Sunday on the front page of the *Times*. By prior agreement, of course, the general's name was not mentioned. I heard the following day that my friend the general was in hot water. President Eisenhower, it seems, was furious because no one had thought to brief or consult *him* on the sweeping changes proposed. Although the conventional wisdom had it that Ike didn't spend much time reading newspapers, he had read the *Times* that weekend. "There was hell to pay," I heard later from a source who must naturally remain anonymous. "The President was Army to the core," he said. "It had been his Army, after all, and he did not take kindly to getting his information about the restructuring plan from the newspaper." When he was called on the carpet, my informative general took refuge in his anonymity. He could not plausibly deny that the restructuring plan existed but insisted he had never talked to me and could not imagine where I had got the information.

To make certain that his tracks were covered, the general took to asking other reporters he met who "this fellow Abel on the *Times*" was. The general must have believed that if enough people heard him ask who I was, they might come to believe that he had never met or talked with me. He was playing the old Washington game of leaking anonymously and then invoking "deniability" when called to account. The stratagem must have worked because he moved up the army ladder before long.

Intricate Patterns

Clearly, the game was being played by much the same rules long before the present generation of Washington reporters was out of knee pants. What historians regard as the first significant news leak in American history—it exposed a secret U.S. arms transaction with France—dates from 1778. In the modern era, especially since the end of World War II, leaks have increasingly become part of the everyday interchange between government officials and the press. A succession of presidents have been frustrated and angry over their inability to stop leaks, no less angry than Ronald Reagan must have been when he said in 1983 that he had "thought of the guillotine" for federal employees who leaked classified information to the press.

Leaks, however, do not always involve the transmission of classified information. Presidents can become just as exercised, as in the case of Lyndon Johnson, when the names of prospective appointees to high office are published or broadcast in advance of a public announcement. Johnson's anger led him to cancel several planned appointments for this reason.

It is not against the law for officials to leak sensitive information, or for reporters to accept and publish such leaks. The notable exception, which can lead to prosecution, has to do with publishing classified information about the government's capacity to eavesdrop on the communications of foreign governments and divulging intelligence gathered by these methods. The entire system of security classification was set up, not by law, but by a series of presidential executive orders, the first of which was issued by President Truman in 1951. The only effective sanction open to the government, seldom invoked as we shall see, is to fire the leaker—if he can be identified. Given the size of the federal bureaucracy and the determination of reporters not to expose their sources, this is not an easy task.

The government's problem with leaks and leakers tends to center on three related areas: foreign policy, defense, and, to a lesser extent, two intelligence organizations, the Central Intelligence Agency and the National Security Agency. There is also the White House itself. For all the presidential anger and frustration over the years, many White House assistants, even some presidents, have been known to leak information that was likely to promote administration policies and purposes. It would be difficult to count on the fingers of one hand the number of significant leaks that came out of the Department of Health and Human Services or the Agriculture Department over a typical twelve-month period.

In both the State and Defense Departments, the information habitually provided to the media through open briefings and press releases tends to be sparse. More than one retired official has conceded in retrospect that serious foreign-affairs journalism would be crippled if reporters did not have access to less closemouthed sources, willing to provide additional information and insight on an informal and confidential basis. It is from private encounters of this sort that leaks sometimes spring. Most often, however, the stories that result from such encounters are regarded by both reporter and source as a useful way to provide the public with more complete, more nuanced information than the State Department or the Pentagon would feel comfortable putting on the record.

But Is It a Leak?

Journalists do not sit around waiting for leaks. Disclosures that look like leaks are often the products of hard work by enterprising newsmen and newswomen. Tom Wicker of *The New York Times* has described them as "often more nearly the result of good work by reporters diligent and intelligent enough to ask the right questions of the right sources at the right time." How that process works has been illustrated in a scenario by Dean Rusk, secretary of state in the Kennedy and Johnson administrations:

> A reporter is leaving the State Department at the end of the day when he sees the Soviet ambassador's car drive up. Figuring that the ambassador has brought a message, the reporter gives the machinery a chance to work, then starts calling around. After being told he's on the wrong track at several offices, he gets to the fellow on Berlin, who has been told never to lie directly to the press. The reporter says, "John, I understand that the Soviet ambassador has just come in with a message on Berlin." So the man says, "Sorry, I can't say a thing about it. Can't help you on that." Ah, he's got it. In the absence of an absolute denial he's on the track. He figures out what the Berlin problem looks like and then calls a friend at the Soviet embassy. "By the way," he says, "what's the attitude of the Soviet Union on this particular point on Berlin?" He listens for a few moments, then he [writes] his story [for] the next morning. . . .The chances are that the president will call the secretary of state and ask, "Who in the hell has been leaking news over at the State Department?"[1]

Dean Rusk does not take a tragic view of that kind of enterprise by intelligent and persistent reporters. His hypothetical example suggests, instead, that it would be a mistake to consider every unauthorized disclosure in the press as the product of a leak. Capable Washington reporters follow the state of play on major issues closely. They read everything they can, and they tend to ask themselves, "What is the next logical move?" Then they work the telephone and the corridors in search of confirmation that their surmise was on target. It's a hit-or-miss business, but, by a process some reporters call triangulation, each succeeding call or conversation brings them closer to the one or more sources who are willing to talk. Of course, the public all too often confuses genuine leaks with this kind of enterprise reporting, which owes little or nothing to deliberate disclosures of classified information by an official or a group pursuing its own interests.

*   *   *

In the pages that follow, I explore the traffic in leaks to determine who the leakers are, their motives for leaking, whose interests they serve, and what role they play in keeping the public informed about the operations of government. I shall weigh the costs and benefits of leaks to both the government and the press. I shall also look into the official Washington obsession with secrecy and how it may sharpen the appetite of many reporters to uncover what the government is trying to hide. Finally, I will put forth some modest suggestions for improving matters, suggestions that demand a more rational assumption of responsibility on the part of both government and press.

2 / A Comparative and Historical Look at Leaks

The enemy must not know where I intend to give battle. For if he does not know where I intend to give battle, he must prepare in a great many places. And when he prepares in a great many places, those I have to fight in any one place will be few.

—*Sun Tzu,* The Art of War

To this day, the impeccable logic of Sun Tzu, dating from the fourth century B.C., defines the attitude of presidents, prime ministers, and military commanders toward unauthorized disclosures of tactical information. From George Washington to Ronald Reagan, American presidents have been troubled by leaks of confidential information that might be of value to an adversary, or to domestic opponents seeking political rather than military advantage. "It is much to be wished," General Washington wrote in 1777, "that our printers were more discreet in many of their publications. We see in almost every paper proclamations or accounts, transmitted by the enemy, of an injurious nature. If some hint of caution could be given to them on the subject, it might be of material service."[1]

In Washington's time, with the War of Independence still to be won, printers were not so self-important as to call themselves journalists. They were mostly poor artisans, few of them educated men. Yet these ink-stained printers of the Revolutionary era shared with present-day investigative reporters a disdain for the hints or cautions of the high and mighty. In defense of their zeal to expose official misconduct, they argued that the people had a need to know what their betters were up to. The contemporary notion that the people have a *right*, as well as a *need*, to know belongs to the twentieth century and is still hotly debated. Although

7

few constitutional lawyers grant the existence of such a right, it remains an article of faith for many if not all modern editors and reporters.

From its infancy, the political culture of the United States has set it apart from other nations, including its closest present-day allies. There is no counterpart elsewhere to the stern injunction written into the First Amendment that Congress shall "make no law" abridging the freedom of the press. This is not to suggest that the American press has been immune throughout history to official prosecution or harassment. There were numerous prosecutions under the Sedition Act of 1798 and only one verdict of "not guilty" was returned. More recently, the Pentagon Papers case went all the way to the Supreme Court before the right of *The New York Times* and *The Washington Post* to publish reports drawn from a leaked copy of that official history of America's Vietnam involvement was upheld in a 6-3 vote.

Both Britain and France, by contrast, have made laws over the years hedging press freedom with a range of restrictions. Britain, for example, has an Official Secrets Act that would not be tolerated in the United States. Few governments in Europe or elsewhere allow reporters to forage for news in the corridors and offices of sensitive government departments, as the United States does every day. Neither the French nor the British press has a long sturdy tradition of investigative reporting, and mainstream journalism in both countries tends to be more protective of national leadership.

A French View

Although the French National Assembly, on August 24, 1789, approved Article XI of the Declaration of the Rights of Man and of Citizen, assuring each citizen the right to "speak, write, print in liberty," exception was made for those who abused "this freedom in cases set forth by law." In France the exceptions are everything. As Jean Marie Auby and Robert Ducos-Adar have written, the law calls for criminal prosecution when a publication is charged with provocation to commit crimes, or publishes offenses against public authorities, official bodies, and protected persons. The more powerful the person, the more protection that is granted, beginning with the president: "...it does not require a precise imputation against honor, nor the presence of profanity, but simply an assault on the dignity or the authority of the President of the Republic." The judiciary has its own protections. Article 26 of the Penal Code bans any material that "casts discredit on a judicial act or decision" or that "aims to strip judicial acts or their authors of the consideration inherent in their function."[2]

These and other restrictions have forced upon the French press a degree of self-censorship. When President Giscard d'Estaing of France accepted a personal gift of diamonds from an African ruler notorious for the gross cruelties he inflicted upon his people, it was the raffish weekly *Canard Enchainé* (not the mainstream papers) that raised the first outcry. After *Le Monde* picked up the story, the government filed criminal charges against that most respected of French newspapers, presumably ignoring *Canard* because it was considered a gadfly. And just as French politicians and journalists saw no grave flaws in Richard Nixon's presidency sufficient to warrant the Watergate crisis, they saw no reason why President Reagan should have been weakened by the exposure of his Iran-contra operation. Perhaps they are more cynical about their leaders than Americans tend to be, all too aware that men in power are corruptible, and less prone to raise moral issues against them.

Turning the Tap

The American press, proud of its First Amendment freedom and determined to root out corruption, found itself in a wrenching confrontation with President Nixon when it uncovered the Watergate scandal. Ronald Reagan's turn came in 1986 when an obscure Beirut weekly triggered the chain of disclosures about the Iran-contra affair. In each case, leaks of closely held information—much of it accurate—were of decisive importance.

The very word "leak" suggests faulty plumbing. While the analogy is imperfect, it bears a relationship to the system for distributing information within the U.S. government. The system will deliver information from one agency to another—and to the public, through the press— at designated times and places—when the government, in effect, opens the tap. There is nothing accidental or covert about the release of information in this fashion. The president holds a news conference, the secretary of state or defense testifies before a congressional committee, the Supreme Court (customarily on Mondays) makes public its current decisions. A spokesman for the Department of Energy or Education makes an announcement, then takes questions from reporters. A glance at the front page of the newspaper, or the evening news on television, is enough to demonstrate that the bulk of government information published day by day falls into this category of authorized, overt disclosure.

Washington leaks, by contrast, are *covert* transactions carried out in strict anonymity. An official decides to share with a particular reporter or news organization a piece of confidential or secret information. The source wants the information out, usually for reasons he will not discuss with the reporter, on condition that his identity is concealed. The leaker's motives may be personal. He may, on the other hand, be leaking on behalf of a special interest or faction within the government. Or he may be passing information along with the knowledge and approval of his superiors. In any event, he will insist upon anonymity. The reporter has no choice but to play the game according to the rules if he wants to go on receiving information from that particular source.

And on to England

The practice is not unique to Washington or the United States. In London, for example, at 4:00 p.m. every working day, the press secretary to Prime Minister Margaret Thatcher meets in the turret of Westminster with some 130 reporters assigned to cover the British government and the House of Commons, the so-called Lobby. Bernard Ingham, Mrs. Thatcher's press secretary, is there to answer questions from the press on various current issues. Nothing he says may be attributed to Ten Downing Street, the prime minister's office and official residence. It is a situation tailor-made for selective leaking to grateful reporters. When the Lobby journalists debated a proposal to change the nonattribution rule in 1986, Ingham threatened to discontinue the sessions. The journalists voted 67-55 to maintain the binding rule of anonymity. A member of the House was moved to say: "There is a room in the turret of Westminster which does not exist in which are held meetings that do not take place." The fiction that no such meeting ever took place protects the government's ability to deny, with some degree of plausibility, that the information reported came from the prime minister's office. This system survives in spite of occasional challenges from news organizations such as *The Independent* in London, which as a matter of conscience refuses to take part in the charade.

A Precedent: Tom Paine and the French Arms Deal

Perhaps the first recorded case of a significant news leak in American history dates from the Revolutionary War. The leaker was Thomas Paine, the celebrated pamphleteer of the American Revolution, who brought to light a covert arrangement under which the hard-pressed American colonists received desperately needed shipments of arms and other military equipment from France.

It was a tale filled with deception. One of the diplomatic agents sent to Europe in search of arms and political support was Arthur Lee, a close friend of Paine's, who initiated secret contacts with the French government to arrange for the shipment of cannon, muskets, boots, and uniforms to America. The Count de Vergennes, foreign minister to King Louis XVI, seized the opportunity to embarrass the British. He encouraged Pierre A. Caron de Beaumarchais, who had met with Lee in London, to set up a trading company for the express purpose of shipping arms to America, ostensibly in exchange for Virginia tobacco. The weapons transfer was to have the appearance of a normal business transaction.

Beaumarchais's company, known as Roderique Hortalez, was set up with one million *livres* of working capital from the French treasury, an impressive sum to which Spain added an unspecified contribution. The French purpose, it can be assumed, was less to help the Americans than to multiply the costs of the war to Britain. One of the French ministers sent to Philadelphia received this frank instruction: "We have never pretended to make of America a useful ally. We have no other object than to deprive Great Britain of that vast continent."[3] The court of Louis XVI was not about to embrace America's frontier republicanism.

Paine had detailed knowledge of the secret negotiations owing to his position as secretary of the Foreign Affairs Committee of the Congress, which gave him access to all incoming intelligence from the network of American agents in Europe.[4] He knew, as many in Congress did not, that a merchant named Silas Deane had been sent to Paris in July 1776, with the title of minister, to handle the French arms shipments initiated by Lee. Deane "was to go to Paris in the guise of a private merchant in search of trade."[5]

Playing that role to the hilt, Deane had arranged with Beaumarchais to appear to buy the weapons. Since he had been promised a 5 percent commission on all the transactions, Deane stood to make a considerable profit if he could persuade Congress that the supplies had to be paid for. The markups were spectacular, oddly reminiscent of those charged by various twentieth-century middlemen on shipments of American weaponry to Iran during the Reagan presidency.

A suspicion that all was not right with the arms deal may have led Congress to order Deane's recall from Paris in 1778, and to keep him cooling his heels in Philadelphia for several months thereafter. On December 5 of that year, the *Pennsylvania Packet* published a bitterly unhappy letter from Deane, addressed "To the Free and Virtuous Citizens of America." He complained that Congress had shut its ears against him and went on to attack Lee for incompetence.

Paine rushed to the defense of his friend Lee in a letter to the same paper, published December 15, 1778, under Paine's familiar pen name, Common Sense. In the letter, he accused Deane of being "uncandid" in his account, rejecting the commissioner's contention that he had been called home to report on the general state of affairs in Europe:

> For however Mr. Deane may chuse [sic] to represent or misrepresent the matter, the truth is that his contracts and engagements in France had so involved and embarrassed Congress that they found it necessary and resolved to recall him, that it ordered him home. . . .[6]

This was to be the first of a fusillade of Paine letters over many months, each followed by letters from Deane's defenders. As the scandal widened, Paine kept adding details drawn, for the most part, from the secret files of the Committee on Foreign Affairs. In his letter of January 2, 1779, Paine started introducing what today would be called "classified information":

> The supplies here alluded to are those which were sent from France in the *Amphitrite, Seine* and *Mercury* about two years ago. They had at first the appearance of a present, but whether so or on credit, the service was nevertheless a great and friendly one. . . .
>
> If Mr. Deane or any other gentleman will procure an order from Congress to inspect an account in my office, or any of

Mr. Deane's friends in Congress will take the trouble to come themselves, I will give him or them my attendance and show them in a handwriting which Mr. Deane is well acquainted with, that the supplies he so pompously plumes himself upon were promised and engaged, and that as a present, before he ever arrived in France, and the part that fell to Mr. Deane was only to see it done. . . .

Paine was, of course, in a questionable position. As a ranking official of the United States, he had taken an oath "well and faithfully to execute the trust reposed in him, according to his best skill and judgment, and to disclose no matter, the knowledge of which shall be acquired in consequence of his office, that he shall be directed to keep secret." His self-serving interpretation of that undertaking left him free to publish whatever he chose so long as he was not explicitly directed to keep the matter secret. Congress, moreover, had taken no step to curb his disclosures.

He was clearly vulnerable to the counterattack launched by one Matthew Clarkson in the *Packet*, on December 31, 1778. Clarkson asked "what business the secretary of the Committee of foreign affairs had to enter into a discussion in the public papers of the character and merits of the ministers of those states at foreign courts, particularly at a time when those matters are under the consideration of Congress, and to boast to the public that he is from the nature of his office acquainted with certain state matters, which are not even known to the *legislatures of these states*." But Paine, undeterred by criticism, kept hammering away. In a Common Sense letter, published January 5, 1779, he revealed that the French court had entered into the arms-supply arrangement while still technically at peace with Great Britain and before concluding its Treaty of Amity and Commerce with the United States on February 6, 1778. The French minister in Philadelphia, Conrad Alexandre Gerard, demanded a formal retraction from Paine and, that failing, addressed himself to Congress. Paine's writings, Gerard insisted, "expose equally the dignity and reputation of the King . . . and that of the United States."

Although Paine had barely hinted at the king's involvement in the arms transaction, and later justified his breach of diplomatic etiquette with the argument that since France had declared war on Great Britain six months earlier he saw no reason to keep the matter secret, Gerard offered to buy Paine's silence with a bribe, which Paine refused.

Gerard's demand that Congress disavow or retract Paine's allegations led to a series of embarrassing delays. It encountered a clear congressional reluctance to deny outright what some prominent members knew to be the truth. Paine had the records to substantiate many of his allegations and members knew him well enough to fear that, if pressed, he would make more damaging revelations.

The American public knew little, beyond rumor, of the wrangling in Congress, which barred the press from its sessions. The Philadelphia papers paid little heed to the weapons story as it filtered out of the closed sessions. Their reporting concentrated instead on the character of various congressmen and, inevitably, of Thomas Paine.

Paine did not wait to be censured. He submitted his resignation on January 8, 1779, later adding: "I have revealed no secrets because I have told nothing that was, or I conceive, ought to be a secret." But that did not end the disputation in Congress. Deane's supporters, ignoring the letter of resignation, insisted upon a retroactive dismissal. The Paine faction countered with demands that he be heard before any action was taken. These motions, too, failed, and Paine never received the hearing his supporters insisted was a matter of right.

Through four days, Congress debated the matter before arriving at a strange resolution. By unanimous vote, Congress resolved that its president, John Jay, should assure Minister Gerard that Congress

> do fully. . .disavow the publications referred to. . . ; and as they are convinced by indisputable evidence that the supplies shipped in the *Amphitrite, Seine* and *Mercury* were not a present and that his most Christian Majesty, the great and generous ally of these United States, did not preface his alliance with any supplies whatever sent to America, so they have not authorized the writer of the said publications to make any such assertions as are contained therein, but on the contrary, do highly disapprove of the same.

The honor of Louis XVI had been saved by an official lie: that the king had sent no military supplies to America before entering into his alliance with the United States. At no point does the text mention Paine by name.

The relevance of Paine's indiscretions to present-day conditions may be questioned. He was, after all, a government official at the time with access to what today would be considered classified information. He printed the information on his own rather than slipping it into the hands of a reporter, as contemporary officials might do. The line is more sharply drawn today between public officials and reporters.

Yet the distinction is less clear than it appears on the surface. Paine disseminated to the public confidential information gained through his position in the government. Any number of former presidents and former secretaries of state have published memoirs based to a considerable extent on classified information to which they had access by virtue of the offices they held. None have been prosecuted, or heavily criticized, for doing what Paine had done. But these latter-day revelations, such as they may have been, were not regarded as leaks. The critical distinction doubtless lay in the fact that Paine was still a government employee when he started disseminating the secrets of the French arms-supply arrangement, causing more embarrassment to the French court at Versailles than to the Congress in Philadelphia.

Paine, in any event, paid a price for his zeal to expose the truth as he knew it. For eight years after his resignation, he lived in poverty, unable to obtain another position. That is more than can be said for officials and journalists who play the game of leaks in Washington today.

Doonesbury

BY GARRY TRUDEAU

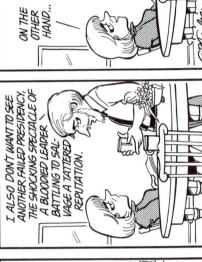

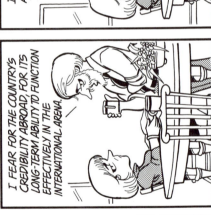

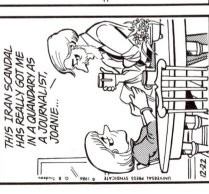

DOONESBURY
COPYRIGHT 1986 G. B. Trudeau.
Reprinted with permission of Universal Press Syndicate. All rights reserved.

3 / Leakers and Their Infinite Variety of Motives

There is a curious delusion among upper bureaucrats and high officials that a reporter cannot possibly reach the same rather obvious conclusions that government officials reached unless the reporter has had illicit access to secret information.

—*Stewart Alsop, in* The Center: People and Power in Political Washington

John F. Kennedy can be credited with the observation that "the Ship of State is the only ship that leaks at the top." The point he was making, though slightly overstated, is widely accepted in Washington to this day. White House press secretaries and spokesmen at the State and Defense Departments seldom play the leaker's game. George Reedy, once press secretary to President Lyndon B. Johnson, has written that "since manipulation of the press involves favoritism to some newsmen it inevitably creates antagonism among others."[1] Civil servants, particularly at the low to middle level, seldom resort to leaking. For them the risk of exposure outweighs the possible gain. Besides, most officials below the policymaking level do not as a rule have access to the kind of information that makes a front-page splash. When a major leak is published, the immediate executive-branch reaction is to blame Capitol Hill. Members of Congress and their staffs tend to be more talkative than administration officials, all the more so when the White House is controlled by one party and the Congress by another. But the fine art of leaking, as Kennedy understood, is most often practiced at the level of the cabinet and subcabinet or among the president's closest advisers in the White House.

Some presidents, notably Jimmy Carter and Ronald Reagan, have been slow to discover that it is their own people, the political appointees, not the bureaucrats, who do much of the leaking. When, for example, Reagan had been in office less than a year, he discussed his concerns about leaks and leakers with Laurence Barrett of *Time*. He said, "there are large layers of the bureaucracy that you cannot change, and there are many of them, I suppose, who are resentful and do not agree with what it is you are trying to do. Now maybe they are the ones that are the principal sources of the leaks."[2] The president, in short, was blaming the permanent government, a cast of characters that does not change with the election returns.

Whether or not Reagan acknowledged the fact, every reporter assigned to the White House during the first term ranked his White House staff as among the most adroit, skillful, and prolific set of leakers since Henry Kissinger presided over the National Security Council staff. Lou Cannon of *The Washington Post*, who has reported on Ronald Reagan since he was governor of California, believes the president himself, without planning it that way, created an atmosphere of policy rivalry that provided subordinates with great incentives to leak. He did it, Cannon believes, by taking inherently contradictory positions on major issues, as when he pushed arms control and the Strategic Defense Initiative, or tax cuts and deficit reduction, at the same time. Each of these policy alternatives had its champions within the upper levels of the administration who would leak classified or confidential information favorable to their side of the argument by way of nudging the president. The leakers were convinced that, by leaking, they were furthering the true objective of the administration.

Why They Leak

Leakers leak for a wide variety of reasons. Stephen Hess, in *The Government/Press Connection*, after studying them, compiled what he calls an "inside government" typology:

> THE EGO LEAK. Passing on information to satisfy the leaker's sense of his own importance. Hess says it is popular with staff-level people, who have fewer outlets than their superiors for ego-tripping. He believes it is the most frequent

cause of leaking, though it may not account for truly major leaks.

Example: Yeoman Charles E. Radford, a navy stenographer assigned to the National Security Council staff, reportedly leaked to Jack Anderson, the syndicated columnist, a sheaf of secret papers revealing President Nixon's determination to "tilt" U.S. policy in favor of Pakistan during its brief war with India in December 1971. Radford, who had been passed over for promotion, also was unhappy over the policy turn against New Delhi, where he had served in the American embassy and made good friends among the Indians.[3]

THE GOODWILL LEAK. Its primary purpose is for the leaker to earn credit with a reporter, to be cashed in at a later date.

Example: David Stockman, director of the Office of Management and Budget in the Reagan administration, sat for eighteen tape-recorded interviews with William Greider of *The Washington Post* over an eight-month period in 1981. The result was a long article in *The Atlantic*, published in the December issue, revealing Stockman's disenchantment with the supply-side doctrine of the administration. He described the Kemp-Roth bill, which embodied the president's tax proposals, as "a Trojan horse to bring down the top rate," that is, to lower tax rates for the wealthy. Of the bargaining that led to the bill's adoption, Stockman was quoted as having said: "Do you realize the greed that came to the forefront? The hogs were really feeding." Why was Stockman talking so freely? Greider later wrote that Stockman may have felt he was getting "a valuable connection with an important newspaper. . .to prod and influence the focus of our coverage."[4] There is no evidence that his cooperation with Greider, then assistant managing editor of the *Post,* paid off in terms of influence with the newspaper, although it did earn him a trip "to the woodshed" with President Reagan.

THE POLICY LEAK. A straightforward pitch for or against a policy proposal, using documents or insider information in hope of getting more attention from the press than the information often warrants. Hess puts the Pentagon Papers leak in this category.

Example: *The Washington Times* published on February 6, 1987, the edited minutes of a National Security Council meeting, held three days earlier, purporting to show that President Reagan was leaning toward early deployment of the Strategic Defense Initiative. Both the newspaper and the journalist who signed the article had been strong advocates of the SDI program.

THE ANIMUS LEAK. Information disclosed for the purpose of embarrassing another person or faction.

Example: Both Alexander Haig, then secretary of state, and Richard Allen, the national security adviser, became targets of leakers within the administration in October and November of 1981. The late Joseph Kraft, for example, devoted his syndicated column of October 27 to rumors of an impending shake-up: Haig would be replaced at the State Department by Caspar Weinberger, who in turn would be succeeded at Defense by Edwin Meese, and William Clark (then Haig's deputy at State) would take Allen's place as national security adviser. Much the same story was broadcast the following day on CBS's "Evening News" by Bob Schieffer. Both Haig and Allen were removed within a year. There is general agreement among reporters that the somewhat premature rumors were planted by hostile sources inside the administration.

THE TRIAL BALLOON. Revealing a proposal that is under consideration to test its eventual reception.

Example: On January 7, 1982, *The New York Times* carried the headline: REAGAN AIDES URGE INCREASE IN TAXES ON CONSUMER ITEMS. The story, by Edward Cowan, said that "President Reagan's economic advisers have reached a consensus that he seek increases in 'consumption taxes,' including those on alcohol, tobacco and gasoline, as part of a strategy to shrink budget deficits in the next few years well below $100 billion. . . ." All Washington knew that the president had consistently opposed any increase. But, as the *Times* reported the following day in a story by Steven

R. Weisman: "White House officials have been working hard in recent weeks to achieve unanimity among themselves on the need for at least some tax increases in 1983 and 1984. Their assumption has been that only with a unified approach could they hope to persuade a reluctant Mr. Reagan to accept tax increases to help reduce the Federal deficit." On January 21, despite warnings by Larry Speakes and David Gergen that nobody knew what the president would do, and that he wanted his aides to stop speculating about his decision, the *Times* reported a Reagan decision in favor of the tax increase. The following day, the *Times* pulled back: "President Reagan appeared to be having second thoughts today." In fact, the president did not propose a tax increase in 1982. It was impossible to deny, however, that the *Times* stories had accurately reflected the views of a majority of his advisers who had tried, and failed, to change his mind. It was a case, wrote Rowland Evans and Robert Novak in their syndicated column, of senior White House aides using the media to pressure the president in a "game of decision-by-leak." If that was the strategy, it certainly failed.

THE WHISTLE-BLOWER. Unlike the other categories, this one is usually the last resort of frustrated civil servants who feel they cannot correct a perceived wrong through regular channels. Whistle-blowing is by no means synonymous with leaking. While leakers demand and get anonymous treatment, some whistle-blowers are willing to state their case in public and risk the loss of their jobs.[5]

Establishing Motive

A leaker's motives are not always apparent to the reporter who receives the information and publishes it. But a good reporter, wise to the ways of Washington, will certainly seek to establish the leaker's motives before going to press. One obvious problem is that motives are not easily teased out and may, in fact, overlap. A policy leak, for example, may also bear the weight of animus, since officials on either side of a policy dispute may at the same time be trying to settle a grudge with their antagonists.

A case in point, cited by Hess and by Martin Linsky in his study titled *Impact*, was Bob Woodward's report in *The Washington Post* of February 19, 1982, concerning remarks attributed to Alexander Haig at a senior staff meeting in the State Department.[6] The Woodward story quoted Haig as having called Lord Carrington, then the British foreign secretary, "a duplicitous bastard." The story, said to be based on the notes of a participant, also revealed that in private conversation with his aides, the secretary of state took a darker view of U.S. prospects in the Middle East than he had taken in public statements. Washington's first and all-but-unanimous reaction was that the notes had been supplied by someone who was trying to undermine or destroy Haig.

Three days later, in his column in *The New York Times*, William Safire came up with a totally different interpretation. According to Safire, Woodward had set out to answer an embarrassing question: "Was it true that Al Haig had gone bonkers?" The leaker, nameless to this day, was a Haig loyalist worried by criticism that the secretary was not sufficiently tough, Safire wrote. Through a careful selection of tough-sounding quotations from his notes, the leaker apparently was trying to demonstrate that Haig was of sound mind and in command of his department. The Safire version is now widely accepted in Washington as the truth, although some reporters consider the motivation of the leaker somewhat irrelevant. All that matters, they say, is that Haig's words were accurately reported.

That is not a view shared by all Washington journalists, although few would go so far as Robert McCloskey, a former State Department spokesman who became the *Post's* ombudsman after retiring from the foreign service. McCloskey denounced the leak as "dishonorable" and the leaker as a "villain." He also criticized Woodward in his own newspaper, arguing that the reporter had an obligation to let the readers know "whether the source's motive was benign or mischievous."

Another example of a leak where the motives are unclear began with the publication of a letter from Secretary Weinberger to President Reagan on the eve of his first summit meeting in Geneva with Mikhail Gorbachev. The letter, dated November 13, 1985, and leaked to the press, was printed three days later in *The New York Times* and summarized in *The Washington Post*. In it, Weinberger warned the president that he would "come under great pressure" from the Soviet leader to make commitments in three areas of arms control. For example, Weinberger wrote, "the Soviets may propose communiqué or other language that obscures their record of arms control violations by referring to the 'importance that both sides attach to compliance. . . .' Language that enables the Soviets to appear equally committed to full compliance—even as they continue to enlarge their pattern of violations—will make the difficult task of responding to those violations even more problematic."[7]

At first glance, the letter looked like a last-minute attempt by Weinberger, who had not been invited to the Geneva meeting, to stiffen the president's back against concessions to Gorbachev. The letter itself did not strike many knowledgeable officials as in any way remarkable. Weinberger's attitude toward arms control was hardly a secret, and there was reason to believe the president agreed with him. The remarkable fact seemed to be that someone had given copies of the letter, together with a report on purported Soviet violations of existing arms-control treaties, to Michael R. Gordon of the *Times* and Walter Pincus of the *Post*. For what purpose?

The *Times* alone published the text, saying no more about the circumstances than that it had received a copy, signed "Cap," from a "source who asked not to be identified." That made it sound like a leak. It seemed clear that someone, some faction, had leaked the letter and the report to put pressure on Reagan, or Weinberger, or both. Was it the faction, centered in the State Department, that wanted to get on with real give-and-take negotiations at Geneva? Or was it the Pentagon faction, supposedly centered in the offices of Fred C. Iklé, under secretary of defense, and Richard N. Perle, assistant secretary for international security policy, that wanted any giving to be done by the Soviets? Here was "a shadowy tale, by golly," as Russell Baker wrote in the *Times* a few days afterward.

Had the letter been published a day or two earlier, it might have caused less fussing and fuming. But it came out the day President Reagan was flying to Geneva. The president, so the *Post* reported, held a mid-air conference with his staff to determine who had leaked the letter. A senior official on board Air Force One was asked by a reporter whether the letter might be an effort to sabotage the summit conference. "Sure it was," the official replied. Another senior official, equally anonymous, was quoted as saying that the unauthorized release of the letter was "a blatant attempt to undermine the president just before the summit." The mystery deepened as the level of official indignation rose.

Upon closer examination, the incident appears to have been vastly overblown. Both Gordon and Pincus had known the violations report was in preparation many days before the president's departure. Both the

Post and the *Times* had mentioned this fact earlier. Pincus and Gordon had been on the lookout for copies of the completed report, although they had no prior knowledge of the cover letter that would be attached to it. They noted that both documents were unclassified, an odd omission for a security-minded administration if it intended to keep the matter secret. The Pentagon, moreover, had scattered copies all over Washington, and Pentagon spokesman Robert B. Sims said that he assumed the officials to whom it was addressed, in turn, had shared the Weinberger letter with subordinates.

The Pentagon went through the motions of ordering an in-house investigation to determine how the letter had found its way into the newspapers, but nothing more was heard of that. Gordon, when asked about his source, argued the question was irrelevant in view of the large number of copies distributed and the fact that neither document had been classified. "I can think of motives for either party [to the arms-control debate] to have leaked it," he said. Whoever the leaker may have been (Gordon will not say), it would be hard to prove that the president's position at Geneva was seriously affected, one way or the other, by the hullabaloo. It would be equally difficult to demonstrate that Secretary Weinberger's position within the administration had been weakened or strengthened. In short, whatever the leaker's motive may have been, his strategy misfired.

Sometimes the leaker's motive is clear, and leaking serves its purpose. A skilled hand was at work when Robert McFarlane, in secret testimony before the Tower Commission, said that he had drafted a document on the night of November 18, 1986, that would have allowed President Reagan to "plausibly deny that he gave prior approval" for the initial sales of arms to Iran, although in fact he had approved it. McFarlane testified on February 19, 1987. *The New York Times* exposed the secret the following morning in a front-page article by Steven B. Roberts, attributing his information to "a source familiar with the [Tower] board's investigation." The White House effort to conceal Mr. Reagan's actual role included a memorandum written by McFarlane at the request of Admiral Poindexter, his successor as national security adviser. The point of the document, according to Roberts's source, "was to permit the president to say no, he didn't give a formal authorization" when he was questioned about it at a news conference the following day. As for the McFarlane memorandum, Roberts's source said, "the president liked it, he was four-square for it from the beginning." Obviously, the source had wasted no time letting the *Times* know of McFarlane's testimony. The source, it turned out, was Leonard Garment, McFarlane's lawyer.

When interviewed about his role, Garment did not deny that he had provided information to the *Times* as well as the *Baltimore Sun* in connection with McFarlane's testimony before both the Tower Commission and the Senate Intelligence Committee. What he did, Garment said, was a little "constructive editing," designed to help the reporter as well as his client. "I wanted people to know what was going on," Garment added. He argued that when reporters had a piece of the story, on some occasions skewed by leaks from less friendly sources, it was his duty to correct the perspective by filling in the missing details. His motive, he said, was to serve the interests of his client, Robert McFarlane.

Leaks from the Right

The story in *The Washington Times* of February 6, 1987, headlined "NSC MINUTES SHOW PRESIDENT LEANING TO SDI DEPLOYMENT," also left no doubt about the motive of the "leaker." The reporter, Gregory A. Fossedal, a media fellow at the Hoover Institution and a contributing editor of *Harper's*, was a strong proponent of the Star Wars program with excellent contacts among advocates of strategic defense. Fossedal apparently enjoyed access to the minutes of a National Security Council meeting on February 3, "obtained without violating the law," as Fossedal wrote. That record, he added, appeared "to show growing sentiment for a move to start construction of a shield against nuclear weapons."

Fossedal, in an interview, declined to answer questions about how he obtained the minutes. He talked in more general terms about the activism of young conservatives like himself. "Here you have a President who made radical proposals in strong rhetoric but some of his policies don't match the rhetoric. On issues like SDI, weapons for the Afghan guerrillas, even tax policy before the tax reform legislation of 1986, you had young conservatives in government who felt passionately that the President was not going far enough. So some of them leaked information designed to hold the President to his proclaimed beliefs. Most leaks in recent years may have been politically embarrassing, but it's hard to think of one that jeopardized national security."

THE PILLSBURY CASE. A typical case in some respects is that of Michael Pillsbury, who was fired from the Defense Department in 1986, allegedly for leaking information to the press about a plan to provide Stinger anti-aircraft missiles to rebel forces in Angola. Pillsbury denied that he was the source of that story. One of his congressional supporters, Senator Gordon J. Humphrey, Republican of New Hampshire, said that Vice Admiral John M. Poindexter, then national security adviser, became annoyed with Pillsbury for "bringing to bear pressure on the White House to improve the quality of weaponry for [the rebel forces in] Afghanistan. He was a burr under the saddle." As assistant under secretary for policy planning in the Defense Department, Pillsbury also was a member of the so-called 208 Committee that oversees covert action. In that role, he is said to have clashed with Lt. Col. Oliver L. North over Nicaragua policy, charging that the marine officer had violated standard procedures. Poindexter accused Pillsbury of leaking classified information, Humphrey said, after a shouting match with North.

Pillsbury, now an adviser on foreign policy and national security affairs to four conservative senators, including Humphrey, is older than many of the young conservative activists who flocked to join the so-called Reagan Revolution. At forty-three, he is also far less predictable. With a doctorate from Columbia University in Chinese studies, he speaks Mandarin and was an early advocate of establishing a military relationship with Beijing to offset the rise of Soviet power. He developed the idea in 1973, when it sounded like heresy to most conservatives, while employed as an analyst by the Rand Corporation. He wrote and sent an article on the subject to Ronald Reagan, then governor of California. Reagan endorsed the idea in 1976, writing Pillsbury: "I am convinced we must strengthen this relationship with China to maintain a balance of power with Russia."[8] In 1985, he also argued forcefully within the Reagan administration for a new approach to India, the largest of nonaligned countries and no favorite of hard-line conservatives. The United States, he said, had too long neglected India, leaving that country chiefly dependent on the Soviet Union for arms supplies.

His proposal to permit U.S. sales of high-technology equipment to India ran into powerful opposition within the government, but his argument prevailed after a contentious three-hour hearing in the office of Fred C. Iklé, under secretary of defense for policy. It was a costly victory, Pillsbury conceded, because his provocative behavior "generated bitterness" against him. "I have a lot to learn about the human dimension of Washington policy struggles," Pillsbury told *The Washington Post.* "But the lessons I have already learned could be put to good use in the Reagan administration and its successors."

"YOU NEVER TALKED TO ME, RIGHT?" One source who needed no instruction in the art of leaking was Lt. Col. North. From the time of the Grenada invasion in 1983, which he helped plan, North made himself an important source of information for a group of reporters from the Associated Press, *The New York Times, Newsweek, Time, Reader's Digest,* National Public Radio, and the Evans and Novak column. He was available and particularly informative in times of crisis, when less daring officials might have gone to ground. Even as he talked with the reporters, North would interject from time to time: "You never talked to me, right?"

Maynard Parker, editor of *Newsweek,* believes that North's readiness to talk with reporters about a wide range of sensitive matters gave him a degree of immunity from probing questions that might have exposed the Iran-contra deal before it became public knowledge thanks to the Beirut leak in November 1986. The press has a bias, Parker acknowledged in a panel discussion at Stanford University, in favor of "sources who see us versus those who do not." He added: "There is no question that scoops [North] provided blunted the intensity of the press instinct for looking into that question. The media committed one of its biggest sins, basically sleeping with our sources, and as a consequence we blew the biggest story of the Reagan Administration."

More than a few of the reporters in North's confidence suspected his deep involvement in the contra-supply effort after Congress had prohibited military assistance, but they did not pursue the story aggressively. *The New York Times,* for example, published a detailed account of North's activities without mentioning his name. As *Newsweek* later speculated: "If more of the reporters who knew him best had decided at that time that North was no longer a source but a big part of the story itself, significant details about the contra-aid operation might have emerged earlier."[9]

The press, in short, runs a double risk in these transactions. Pursuing its self-interest in leaks, which serves to advance the career aspirations of reporters and the prestige of their organizations, the press risks some sacrifice of independent judgment. It can be lulled into treating government sources that make secret information available more favorably than it treats reluctant sources. To the extent that reporters wind up in bed with their sources, their motives may be no less questionable than those of the politicians and bureaucrats who do the leaking.

No Discipline on the Right

There is general agreement among Washington reporters and editors that the volume of leaks has risen from a trickle to a torrent over the past decade. "They run in cycles," said Laurence Barrett of *Time*, "which are directly related to the amount of stress within an administration." Dom Bonafede, a veteran journalist now teaching at American University, explained the present-day flood of leaks in terms of a competition among individuals and factions for access to the public mind. "Government people are more savvy today," he said, "and far more aware of the importance of putting their case before the public through the press. The practice is probably amoral but in the present climate it is also indispensable and endemic. A leak today no longer means that someone has dumped a sheaf of government papers over the transom." Both leakers and reporters, Bonafede added, have become more sophisticated: "Sometimes a word over the telephone or a gesture made in a face-to-face encounter will do it."

Several of the correspondents interviewed traced the increase in leaking to the cavalier attitude of far-right officeholders toward traditional government procedures. Some called it a lack of discipline. "One reason this administration lacks discipline is that there are so many ideologues on board, who believe they are responding to a higher calling. They came to Washington to make a revolution and they simply don't believe in government and its rules" said John Walcott of *The Wall Street Journal*. A similar view was expressed by Daniel Schorr of National Public Radio, who, like Walcott, has been the recipient of a great many leaks over the years. "A large number of leaks," he said, "come from right-wing ideological types, who are fundamentally contemptuous of government."

Nothing New Under the Sun

It would be naive to suggest that ideology came to Washington with the Reagan administration. In many ways, however, the United States enjoyed a broad foreign-policy consensus from the Truman years through the Eisenhower and Kennedy administrations. Such major policy departures as America's decision to join the United Nations as a founding member, the Marshall Plan for European recovery, the establishment of the North Atlantic Treaty Organization, the Korean War, even the early involvement in Vietnam, had broad bipartisan support. Powerful congressional leaders such as House Speaker Sam Rayburn and Lyndon B. Johnson, as majority leader of the Senate, maintained party discipline. The fundamental policies of the cold war era were not seriously challenged until the late 1960s and early 1970s, as the Vietnam fighting dragged on with mounting casualties and no end in sight. The Watergate affair, leading to the resignation of President Nixon, also cast the press in a new and more aggressive role. The notion of the American press as the fourth branch of government now seemed out of date as reporters increasingly came to question the wisdom of national leadership.

The career of James Reston, the patriarch of *The New York Times* in Washington, illustrates the distinctly different ways in which Washington reporters went about their work during the consensus years. By his own description, Reston was a "scoop artist" as a young man. He attributes his first great scoop, a remarkably accurate series of articles on the emerging shape of the United Nations Charter, to a stroke of blind luck. Reston was new to Washington, and had yet to acquire many high-powered sources, when the great powers of World War II assembled at Dumbarton Oaks to write the charter. He soon struck gold.

As the sessions were being conducted in elaborate secrecy, Reston's informed articles provoked envy and gossip among his competitors. Some suspected that the British delegation, headed by Sir Alexander Cadogan, was leaking documents to Reston. Others guessed that the leakers were State Department people, who were believed to harbor a bias in favor of the *Times*. Both wrong, Reston said in an interview. His source was an obscure and distinctly junior member of the Chinese delegation. The young Chinese introduced himself and, as the conference went on, he delivered to Reston a succession of secret working papers and other documents. "It turned out," Reston recalled, "that some years earlier my young friend had worked at the *Times* in New York as a copy boy. He felt obligated to the *Times* for having given him the job."

Reston managed to score many other scoops over the years by playing his cards shrewdly. When he learned that J. Robert Oppenheimer was in trouble with the Atomic Energy Commission over his security clearance, he went into action quickly. As director of the Los Alamos laboratory at the time the atomic bomb was developed, and after the war as a consultant to the government, Oppenheimer was a greatly admired scientist. The news that he was to be stripped of his clearance seemed to Reston a story the *Times* was uniquely equipped to handle. He went to Princeton, New Jersey, where Oppenheimer was director of the Institute for Advanced Study. "I persuaded Oppie and Lloyd Garrison, his lawyer, that they would be better served by releasing the story to the *Times*" rather than waiting for the government to announce it, Reston said.

Reston's chief competitor in the postwar years was Joseph Alsop, the syndicated columnist of the *New York Herald Tribune*. Alsop, now retired and living in Georgetown, had his share of exclusive reports. Looking back on those active and successful years, he said : "I never had access to classified papers. I didn't seek them. I knew everybody in those days; I would see four people a day, listen and ask questions. The important thing was the preparation. I would swot before each interview to make sure I knew enough to ask intelligent questions."

Bridging the Generations

Richard Harwood, assistant managing editor of *The Washington Post*, bridges the gap between the Alsop/Reston generation and the *Post's* youthful investigative reporters of the 1980s. "What's a leak?" he said. "From the government standpoint it's a premature disclosure of a new appointment, a policy decision or of classified information. The usual motivation of the leaker is to influence policy or to wound an adversary. I suppose we've always had leaks in times of great tension but they have proliferated now. There are historical reasons, I suppose, like the collapse of the postwar consensus. The new breed of young reporters is very talented, very hard-working. Also, editors now are willing to print things they would not have touched 20 years ago."

Although the ethics of leaking, and accepting leaks, are much discussed in Washington, few reporters offer hard answers or clear definitions. Harwood mentioned an incident back in 1982 or 1983 that raised a puzzling question for him. A *Post* reporter had been told by a congressional staff assistant that the CIA was financing the Nicaraguan rebels. *Post* editors decided they could not publish a story based on hearsay. They asked for strong confirmation. "We ran a check with a CIA official, who said, 'Yes, it's true, but don't quote me,'" Harwood recalled. "I kept asking myself, which was the leak—the tip from the staff fellow on the Hill or the anonymous confirmation from the CIA man? We ran the story. But it's still hard to tell a leak from a plant."

Hodding Carter, a Mississippi editor who served as State Department spokesman in the Carter administration, has seen the ethical dilemma from both sides. In an interview with Philip Geyelin, syndicated columnist and editor in residence at the School of Advanced International Studies of Johns Hopkins University, Carter, talking as a former government official, deplored excessive secrecy:

> . . . I think that even now you could knock off about 80 percent of it and suffer nothing at all. . . .the classification stuff—it's ridiculous. What's silly about it is that because everything is classified folks feel perfectly free to abuse their responsibility in the leaking of stuff that they shouldn't be leaking. . . .I'm occasionally horrified by things that are leaked, though I must say that to blame anyone except ourselves is silly. The greatest offenders in this town come from the White House, Defense and State. We don't have to be worrying about any moles.

Carter, the journalist, reasserted himself when talking about his distaste for reporters who allow themselves to be used by officials for their own purposes. He called it "clientitis." What he meant was "taking stuff that is fed out and, as a condition for getting it, using it without question—neither identifying the source so that somebody can place where the information fits into the debate, nor going around [to other sources] and trying to balance it off."

Carter believes that good journalism involving classified information is possible even though it starts from a leak or a hint, but that it necessarily calls for hard work by the reporters. "I saw some good stories that were the result of piecing together material and then going to somebody and getting the final piece," Carter said. "They almost always started with something being handed over and going on from there. Often, you know, reporters in this town are good enough that it doesn't take much more than just one hint to get them in right direction. Everybody knows that's all it takes, which is why there will always be leaks."[10]

4 / Purposeful Disclosure

This leaking has got to stop. . . . If there are any leaks out of your area, whatever the area may be, I am going to fire you. Whether or not that's fair, and I can see where some of you might not think it fair, this has just got to stop.

—*Jimmy Carter to a meeting of State Department officials,*
February 6, 1979

Every president since World War II has been troubled by leaks of government secrets and, in some cases, of classified documents. In their largely unsuccessful efforts to control this traffic, successive administrations have ordered the Federal Bureau of Investigation to pry into the lives of reporters and suspected official leakers: telephones have been tapped, polygraph tests administered, and from time to time suspected sinners have been dismissed from government service by way of making an example. Yet the traffic in leaks flourishes and can be expected to plague future presidents so long as policy disputes and tensions persist within their official families.

That the government has been anything but consistent about honoring its own classification system is as clear from the Fossedal story as it was twenty-five years ago, when Max Frankel, executive editor of *The New York Times,* was a young Washington reporter. In August 1961, when the Berlin Wall went up, the White House used the event to try to demonstrate President Kennedy's "toughness" under pressure, at least in rhetorical terms. Ignoring the sensitive nature of the material, the White House made available to Frankel, for direct quotation, certain choice exchanges from a harsh confrontation between Kennedy and An-

33

drei Gromyko, the Soviet foreign minister. The following year, at the
height of the Cuban missile crisis, a State Department official allowed
Frankel to make verbatim notes of another presidential meeting with
Gromyko from the secret official transcript—if the *Times* would agree
not to use direct quotations. The guiding principle, then and now, is
that when it suits an administration's purpose to leak secret information
to the press, it simply ignores or temporarily overrides a document's
classification.

Frankel cited these authorized disclosures, among others, in a deposition on the Pentagon Papers case some nine years later. He argued that
by Washington standards, the notion of secrecy being essential to the
conduct of diplomatic and military affairs was "antiquated, quaint and
romantic." The heart of his case was this:

> . . . practically everything that our government does, plans,
> thinks, hears and contemplates in the realms of foreign policy
> is stamped and treated as secret—and then unraveled by that
> same government, by the Congress and by the press in one
> continuing round of professional and social contacts, and
> cooperative and competitive exchanges of information.
>
> The governmental, political and personal interests of the
> participants are inseparable in this process. Presidents make
> "secret" decisions only to reveal them for the purposes of
> frightening an adversary nation, wooing a friendly electorate,
> protecting their reputations. The military services conduct
> "secret" research in weaponry only to reveal it for the pur-
> pose of enhancing their budgets, appearing superior or in-
> ferior to a foreign army, gaining the vote of a congressman
> or the favor of a contractor. . . . High officials of the govern-
> ment reveal secrets in the search for support of their policies,
> or to help sabotage the plans and policies of rival departments.
> Middle-rank officials of government reveal secrets so as to
> attract the attention of their superiors, or to lobby against the
> orders of those superiors. . . .
>
> This is the coin of our business and of the officials with
> whom we regularly deal. In almost every case, it is secret
> information and, much of the time, it is top secret. But the
> good reporter. . . gains access to such information and such
> sources because they wish to use him for *loyal* purposes of

government while he wishes to use *them* to learn what he can in the service of his readers. Learning always to trust each other to some extent, and never to trust each other fully—for their purposes are often contradictory or downright antagonistic—the reporter and the official trespass regularly, customarily, easily and unselfconsciously (even unconsciously) through what they both know to be official "secrets." The reporter knows always to protect his sources and is expected to protect military secrets about troop movements and the like. He also learns to cross-check his information and to nurse it until an insight or story has turned ripe. The official knows, if he wishes to preserve this valuable channel and outlet, to protect his credibility and the deeper purpose that he is trying to serve.[1]

A Political Instrument

It should be clear from the testimony of Frankel and other experienced Washington correspondents that, contrary to public perceptions, leaking is only seldom the province of the dissident. Richard Halloran, the *Times*'s Pentagon man, calls leaking

> a political instrument wielded almost daily by senior officials within the Administration to influence a decision, to promote policy, to persuade Congress and to signal foreign governments. Leaks are oil in the machinery of government.
> They are also one way the government communicates with itself. A White House assistant, frustrated because he can't get his views before the President, judiciously plants a story likely to catch the President's eye. A Presidential aide, afraid to confront the President directly with bad news, gets his message across through the press. A Cabinet officer, unable to get past the White House palace guard, leaks a memo that will land on the President's desk in the morning newspaper.[2]

Zbigniew Brzezinski, President Carter's national security adviser, acknowledged in an interview that he had shared highly classified information with a small trusted circle of reporters. He insisted, however, that the word "leak" did not apply in such cases, because his were authorized disclosures "for explicit administration purposes." Brzezinski's distinction is uniquely his own. One example he cited involved a carefully orchestrated campaign in late 1980 to warn the Soviet Union against armed intervention in Poland during the Solidarity crisis. He passed along to several reporters detailed intelligence to the effect that the Soviets were massing troops, reports suggestive of imminent intervention. By normal Washington standards, if not by Brzezinski's, this was a clear leak of classified information.

Another official of the Carter administration, Assistant Secretary of Defense Thomas Ross, who was once a reporter, has seen both the usefulness and cost of leaks. In his experience many political appointees in a position to leak did so when it suited their purpose, Ross said, although their purpose was not always clear. In an interview, he acknowledged that he did some leaking himself with the full authorization of his boss, Defense Secretary Harold Brown:

> I knew which of the Pentagon correspondents could be trusted and I had the authority to declassify particular pieces of information when that seemed necessary. . . . Frequently I would leak to counter the effect of a prior leak, you might call that an anti-leak leak, designed to correct the perspective on a story.

Ross has also had to grapple with the consequences of leaks that in some cases were "truly damaging." He cited a column by Rowland Evans and Robert Novak about alleged Soviet violation of the Salt I Treaty. "They even published map coordinates although the evidence we had was far from clear-cut," Ross said. The Russians promptly camouflaged the installation. "When it's a case of exposing the Soviets, the leaks normally come from right-wing sources," Ross said.

Disinformation, Washington Style

A notably misleading series of Washington leaks started with a front-page story in *The Wall Street Journal,* published August 25, 1986, reporting that the United States and Libya were "on a collision course again." Citing U.S. and West European intelligence officials as its sources, the *Journal* reported that the April bombing attacks on Tripoli and Benghazi had not brought an end to Libyan terrorism. "Right now, the

Pentagon is completing plans for a new and larger bombing of Libya in case the president orders it." The story added that new air strikes could be expected to target Libyan oil terminals and other economic installations.

On October 2, Bob Woodward in *The Washington Post* demolished the *Journal* story, acknowledging that the *Post* and several other papers also had carried it in August. Each of them, he wrote, had published false information as fact. He claimed that, according to "informed sources and documents," which he did not further identify, the story had been the product of "a secret and unusual campaign of deception designed to convince Libyan leader Moammar Gadhafi that he was about to be attacked again by U.S. bombers and perhaps ousted in a coup."

Woodward quoted from what he described as a three-page memorandum, written by John M. Poindexter, the president's national security adviser, outlining a new strategy of disinformation. One of its key elements, Poindexter is said to have written, "is that it combines real and illusionary events—through a disinformation program—with the basic goal of making Gadhafi *think* [the word underlined] that there is a high degree of internal opposition to him within Libya, that his key trusted aides are disloyal, that the U.S. is about to move against him militarily." The plan's objective, according to the *Post* account, was to keep Gadhafi "preoccupied" and "off balance" and to portray him as "paranoid and ineffective" so that "forces within Libya which desire his overthrow will be emboldened to take action."

Questioned about the Woodward story at a news conference, President Reagan promptly denied that the plan he had approved in August involved the surreptitious use of American media to spread "disinformation." The denial lost its force, however, when the president added that he wanted Gadhafi to "go to bed every night wondering what we might do." The uproar that followed, notably among American editors and editorial writers who thought of disinformation as a uniquely wicked *Soviet* technique, missed one critical point: that leaks can be a dubious gift to the press even in the United States.

The managing editor of *The Wall Street Journal,* Norman Pearlstine, issued a defensive statement: "If our government. . . mounted a complex disinformation campaign, involving multiple sources here and abroad aimed at the U.S. press, we knew nothing about it. If, indeed, our government conducted such a domestic disinformation campaign, we were among its many victims."

Another case of disinformation involved a document passed to George Wilson, the Pentagon correspondent of *The Washington Post*, during the 1980 election. It took the form of a memorandum, ostensibly addressed to the director of Central Intelligence, warning that 60 percent of the embassy hostages in Teheran would be killed if a rescue by helicopter were attempted. The document purported to be an internal CIA study. It was dated a month before the actual hostage rescue mission failed. The clear inference was that President Carter, then seeking re-election to a second term, had recklessly ordered the rescue attempt in spite of the warning. Wilson did not rush into print with the story. He checked it with the Pentagon and the CIA, and both pointed out that the code name for the rescue operation was wrong. After investigating the document, Frank Carlucci, then deputy director of the CIA, labeled it a forgery.

On Wilson's advice, the *Post* refused to publish the story. On November 16, however, after the election, the paper did carry a Jack Anderson column headlined: "Desert One: Doomed from the Start." It more than faintly resembled the story George Wilson had received from a telephone caller he knew only as "Lloyd," who when pressed for documentation had mailed to Wilson "a plain manila envelope with an out-of-town postmark and a return address that did not check out as real." The Anderson column said: "If the mission had proceeded, as scheduled, from Desert One to a mountain hideout east of Teheran and then on to the actual rescue, the prospects were even more grim. The CIA estimated informally that there would be 60 percent losses among the hostages—in other words about 30 of them would die."

"Lloyd," apparently, had not taken the *Post's* rejection lying down. Wilson, in turn, did not tell the full story until some three years later, after Jody Powell, former press secretary to President Carter, had challenged Anderson's version in his own newspaper column. "Powell vs. Anderson goes beyond the entertainment of two columnists fighting in print," Wilson wrote in an Op-Ed page article published September 23, 1983. The article continued:

> It raises anew the question of whether our checks and balances
> in the press are adequate, given the persistence and sophistica-
> tion of a seemingly growing number of disinformers in an
> age of instant worldwide communication, where the damage

can be fatal—politically or worse. The problem is aggravated by the fact that newspapers. . .often are so big that one news department prints something that another has found flawed, as was the case with the *Post* when it came to the fabricated document.

A Deplorable Tendency

Albert Hunt, *The Wall Street Journal*'s bureau chief in Washington, acknowledged in an interview that reporters generally, his own staff included, "don't work hard enough to indicate the leaker has an axe to grind. We must identify the leaker's bias." Jack Nelson of the *Los Angeles Times* spoke of "a deplorable tendency for reporters to prefer anonymous sources, even when they are willing to be named." Laurence Barrett of *Time* magazine attributed professional lapses of this kind to "the pointless competition to be first with the story. If the press spent half as much time as it invests in these stories trying to find out *why* things happen, the public and our own conscience would be better served."

The intelligent reader is bound to nod in agreement with these sentiments. Of course, leakers have a bias that is too often concealed from the reader. Of course, reporters need to work harder at naming sources. Of course, they should aim at getting the story right, not just at getting it ahead of the competition. The stubborn fact, however, is that newsmen thrive on competition, that editors frequently hesitate to press a reporter to name his sources, and that the public may well find much of the Washington news confusing, even when it is not misleading.

When a reporter accepts a leak and publishes it he is engaging in a transaction based on mutual trust. The reporter must believe that the information he has received is trustworthy, and the leaker must believe that the reporter, in turn, can be trusted to protect the anonymity of his source. It is not, however, a relationship of equals. The reporter risks his reputation when he passes along unverified, sometimes unverifiable, information to the public. If the information turns out to be false or distorted, there is no refuge for the reporter in anonymity.

He can try to protect his own integrity through a decent skepticism about the motive of the leaker. This means cross-checking his information with alternative sources. It also means he must be prepared to abandon the story when it does not check out, which happens every day in

Washington. The real difficulty comes when government officials at a high level pass along information they know to be false.

Protecting National Security

As a group, reporters assigned to the Pentagon show a nice regard for the government's need to keep certain categories of information secret. Charles Bierbauer of the Cable News Network spoke for many of them in a conference on March 1, 1984: "I would accept that there are issues of national security that need to be protected," he said. "And I do not see any reason for me to report on what the targeting of our missiles might be, or what our precise war strategy may be, information which the Soviet Union might surely want to know....On the other hand, if there are weapons systems which do not work, if there are weapons systems which cost billions of dollars far and above what they have been programmed to cost, then I think you would want to know about such systems because you are paying for them and I am paying for them."[3]

Walter S. Mossberg of *The Wall Street Journal*, speaking at the same conference, drew attention to the fact that reports of mismanagement in the defense program were being discouraged, in one case by retroactive reclassification of documents that might be politically embarrassing but had little to do with national security. "I have," he said, "received leaks of numerous classified documents by officials of this [Reagan] administration and others when it suited their political purposes. But if I printed something from other documents, documents that were leaked to me by someone who was in opposition to the...policy of the moment, then I would be accused of violating national security. It is a double standard. It has much more to do with political embarrassment than with anything else. And I fear it is getting worse."[4]

A relevant example cited by Mossberg was his discovery that Egyptian American Transport & Services Corporation (Eatsco), a company hastily organized by Hussein K. Salem, an Egyptian businessman, and Thomas G. Clines, a former CIA official, had received some $71 million in payments from the U.S. Treasury for handling shipments of weapons to Egypt. The money came from long-term American loans to Egypt. Pentagon policy normally bars the use of American loan funds to cover shipping costs. The rules were bent, Mossberg learned from Pentagon officials, because Salem had the blessing of the Egyptian government and the Carter administration wanted to please President Anwar Sadat.

There were other intriguing details: Federal prosecutors were investigating possible ties between Eatsco and Edwin P. Wilson, another former CIA man later convicted on charges of illegally supplying arms to Libya. Wilson had arranged a $500,000 loan in 1979 for Clines. The prosecutors were also looking into the affairs of two Defense Department officials—air force major general Richard V. Secord and Erich F. von Marbod, now retired—who helped oversee the arms sales to Egypt. General Secord's name has figured more recently in the Iran-contra affair.

When Mossberg applied under the Freedom of Information Act for a batch of routine shipping invoices, they were promptly classified. "Under pressure from both the Justice and State departments," Mossberg and Edward T. Pound reported, "the Pentagon has refused to let *The Wall Street Journal* see the more than 20,000 documents it held relating to Eatsco, and it has stopped answering even routine press questions on the subject."

Reagan Cracks Down

The Reagan administration has tried diligently to police contacts between officials and reporters, hoping to stem leaks from inside the executive branch. On January 12, 1982, Reagan signed a directive which required that "all contacts with any element of the news media in which classified National Security matters or classified intelligence are discussed" must have advance approval from a "senior official." The directive also required that the officials interviewed provide a memorandum detailing the issues discussed. As the new rules were announced, an unidentified official added that the directive flowed from "a virtual hemorrhage of leaks in the national security area which the president believes have hampered formulation of foreign and defense policy." Only one example was cited: reports on a decision about fighter planes for Taiwan.

William Clark, then the president's newly appointed national security adviser and a former chief justice of the California Supreme Court, said on that occasion: "We fully recognize the paradox inherent in our system." Stressing that he meant no criticism of the press, Clark added: "The press has been doing its job—collecting information—better than the government has been doing its job—protecting national security information."

The decision to crack down coincided with an order by Frank Carlucci, then Caspar Weinberger's deputy at the Pentagon, that some twenty-five officials who had taken part in a meeting of the Defense Resources Board submit to polygraph tests. To set an example, Carlucci took the test himself after *The Washington Post* published the substance of a classified document considered by the board a few days earlier. According to that document, the joint chiefs of staff had estimated that Reagan's defense buildup would cost the country $750 billion more than the $1.5 trillion projected earlier over a five-year period. It was not the kind of story that compromised intelligence sources and methods or in any way damaged foreign policy decisions. When a Pentagon spokesman was asked why the publication of these figures was considered so sensitive as to warrant wholesale lie detector tests, he lamely acknowledged that there had been no breach of national security. "What is so upsetting to us," he said, was that "someone on the team" had talked out of turn.

Within three weeks the administration backed off. Judge Clark issued a new directive in February omitting any mention of controls on interviews. He also dropped any trace of his earlier threat to use "all legal methods" in tracking down the sources of leaks. All that survived from the original directive was a commitment to reduce the number of officials with access to classified data from the National Security Council.

Leaks continued to flow, and the administration drafted new proposals for punishing suspected officials, including a plan for more extensive polygraph testing. That scheme also foundered when Secretary of State George Shultz said he for one would refuse to be tested. It was not until the spring of 1986 that the administration actually fired two officials on suspicion of leaking—Michael Pillsbury in April and Spencer C. Warren, a State Department speech writer, in May. Both were conservatives apparently dissatisfied with current Reagan policies.

Leaks had long been a weapon in Washington battles between high officials competing for influence over one president or another. Henry Kissinger used them virtuoso-fashion against cabinet rivals in the Nixon administration. Zbigniew Brzezinski, while national security adviser in the Carter administration, was not backward about leaking to undermine Secretary of State Cyrus R. Vance. The Reagan administration now found itself the target of ideological leaks by far-right conservatives, in middle-level positions, who felt their views were being frozen out of the policy process.

An Authorized Leak

All leaks have a purpose. There is a distinction, however, between disclosures authorized on high authority and those lacking authorization. Consider the experience of John P. Wallach of the Hearst News Service. Some weeks before the bombing of Libya by American planes in 1986, Wallach received a tip from a colleague in London. He put in calls to the State Department, the Pentagon, and the White House. In each case he asked the same question: Was it true that Prime Minister Margaret Thatcher had refused to allow U.S. bombers based in Britain to be used in a strike against Libya? The first two officials Wallach reached said they were under a "tight lid," meaning that they had been ordered to say nothing. The third said Wallach's tip was wrong and added helpfully, "The president has decided to act." Source number three also declined to deny Wallach's suggestion that air force F-111 planes would be sent against Libyan targets, thus confirming the reporter's guess.

The direct result of Wallach's investigation was a front-page story quoting a senior administration source to the effect that the British government had given permission for the F-111 strike. It was published on April 12, nearly seventy-two hours before the actual attack. The administration did not protest this disclosure of highly sensitive information about a military operation that had yet to be launched, nor was there a search to identify the leaker. It was a different story when *The Washington Post* and the Evans-Novak column reported that William J. Casey had flown to Angola to arrange for the covert shipment through neighboring Zaire of anti-aircraft missiles to the Angolan guerrilla forces. Michael Pillsbury, the suspected leaker, was promptly required to take a polygraph test, which he failed, bringing his dismissal from the Defense Department.

The difference was that Wallach's story had been authorized. The administration at the time was waging psychological warfare against the Libyan leader, Col. Moammar Gadhafi, through a series of public and private warnings that an attack was coming. The Angola leak had not been authorized. It was viewed as damaging because the story mentioned Zaire, whose government did not wish to be linked with the Angolan insurgent forces of Jonas Savimbi, who in turn was being denounced in Africa for accepting support from South Africa.

While the Reagan administration has continued to crack down on reporters and suspected leakers with indifferent success, knowledgeable officials concede that its efforts have been directed for the most part against leaks that were political embarrassments rather than national security violations. The truly damaging recent breaches of security were the work of government employees who, for a variety of personal reasons, turned out to be spies for the Soviet Union. Compared with these professional agents, the disclosures made by the press were small potatoes.

5 / When Is a Secret a Secret?

If you live and work as a journalist in Washington long enough, several things about national security and the press become self-evident—and they are not always life, liberty and the pursuit of happiness. The first thing you learn is that it is impossible, not just improbable. . .to do your daily job without bumping into a secret.

—*Howard Simons, former managing editor,* The Washington Post

Justice Potter Stewart once observed that when everything is stamped secret nothing is secret. A workable system for protecting state secrets, in short, must be able to discriminate between the trivial and the essential. The United States has no such system.

According to a congressional estimate, the federal government now routinely classifies some 20 million documents a year. Of this mountain of paper, some 350,000 documents are stamped top secret, a classification that means "exceptionally grave damage" would result from their disclosure. A staff study on The Protection of National Secrets, issued in 1985 by the House Judiciary Subcommittee and the Post Office and Civil Service Subcommittee, called for basic reform of the system. Its principal recommendation was that the government sharply reduce the number of documents it wishes to keep secret and, at the same time, sharply reduce the number of officials with access to truly essential defense secrets.

"Only a fraction of the information classified is of a military nature and of value to the Soviets," the report held. "Much material is classified to protect diplomatic relationships, hide bargaining positions, or prevent premature disclosure. All too often, documents are classified to protect politically embarrassing information or to hide government misconduct. . . .

"With so much information classified, even the most routine work requires a security clearance. At the same time, high-level officials cynically ignore the classification designation when it is to their political advantage to do so. . . ."

The weight of numbers overwhelms the system. More than four million Americans now hold security clearances. Those cleared for top secret are supposed to be reinvestigated every five years, but the process is limping ten to fifteen years behind schedule. There is reason also to question the quality of these reinvestigations. The staff study noted that a member of the John Walker spy ring was rechecked twice during fifteen years of undercover work for the Soviet Union. Each time the navy reissued his clearance to handle top secret data.

Starting with the cold war, background investigations were based on an assumption that is widely questioned today: that Americans who betray their country's secrets tend to be Communists, or have Communist associations, men and women driven by ideological commitment to the Soviet Union. The congressional study found instead that in a string of recent, unquestionably damaging, cases of espionage, the American agents had been motivated by greed, financial difficulties, alienation, anger, or lust for excitement. John Walker, for example, was a member of the John Birch Society. William Kampiles, a CIA employee, sold the Russians a technical manual detailing the KH-11 satellite surveillance system; he was unhappy with his assigned job, and his request for a transfer had been turned down. Ronald W. Pelton had declared personal bankruptcy and resigned his $24,500-a-year job at the National Security Agency (NSA) when he sold the Soviet Union the secret of Ivy Bells, a project for eavesdropping on Soviet communications by U.S. submarines.

Drawing the Line

The report also draws a clear, sharp line between "the selling or giving of secret information to an enemy nation"—that is espionage—and "providing secret information to unauthorized persons, including reporters for *The Washington Post*, for the purpose of affecting policy debates"—that is leaking. In the recent case of Samuel Loring Morison, the government may have confused the two categories. Morison was prosecuted for mailing three satellite photographs of a nuclear-powered Soviet aircraft carrier under construction to *Jane's Defence Weekly* in England. A Baltimore jury found Morison guilty on two charges of espionage and two counts of theft, although the government made no claim that the photographs, or the copy of a classified newsletter found in his apartment, were ever seen by the Soviet Union. Morison did not contest the charge that he sent the photographs or that he had possession of the newsletter. The single issue before the jury was to determine whether his actions had caused potential damage to the United States or given the Soviet Union a potential advantage. The prosecution argued that it was potentially helpful to the Soviet Union to know that the KH-11 satellite was operating in 1984—and that it was targeted against projects like the new carrier—also that, but for the published photographs in *Jane's*, the Russians could not have been certain of the satellite's capabilities.

Roland S. Inlow, a retired CIA official who had worked on the targeting of KH-11, testified for the defense although he had no sympathy for Morison's action. He told the court that in his opinion the three photographs printed in *Jane's Defence Weekly* would not have caused damage or injury to the United States. From the photographs, Inlow said, the Soviets could not have learned more than they already knew about the characteristics of the imaging satellite. He reminded the jurors that Kampiles had delivered the technical manual of the KH-11 system to the Russians six years earlier. He added that KH-11 photographs also had been found and published by Iran in 1981 after the failed hostage-rescue mission.

It was no great secret, moreover, that the United States knew about the Soviet carrier under construction. Government officials had talked about it openly for several years, and the unclassified 1984 edition of *Soviet Military Power*, an overt Pentagon publication, had published detailed drawings of the carrier and of the Black Sea shipyard where it was being built.

The jury in the Morison case had an "impossibly difficult task" in trying to decide where the truth lay, Inlow later wrote. "From my perspective, the judicial process seemed heavily tilted in favor of the government. I think the jury was overwhelmed by the complexities of the case in the one area that was being contested. I have great sympathy for the jury. . . . It did the best it could."[1]

Inlow added: "Morison clearly had committed a misdeed; but what he did was not 'espionage.'" Morison, who appealed the guilty verdict, in fact transmitted classified information to a British publication. By any reasonable standard, he was a leaker, not a spy.

A Message to Gadhafi

The government at times appears to play a double game, with one agency wanting to keep material secret for security reasons, another determined to release it for propaganda purposes. The problem often involves intelligence obtained through intercepting coded messages of unfriendly foreign regimes.

On April 4, 1986, for example, the United States is said to have intercepted a message from the Libyan People's Bureau in East Berlin to headquarters in Tripoli telling the Libyan authorities they would be "very happy when you see the headlines tomorrow." A few hours later, according to *Newsweek* and *The Washington Post*, a second message was intercepted to the effect that an operation was "happening now" and would not be traceable to the People's Bureau. The second message was said to have been sent within ten minutes of the bombing at a West Berlin discotheque known as La Belle, which killed an American soldier and a Turkish woman, injuring more than two hundred others.

The intercepted messages, though faintly ambiguous, appeared to justify a conclusion in Washington that Libyan agents operating out of East Berlin had planted the bomb at La Belle. Richard Burt, the ambassador to West Germany, lost no time in claiming an intelligence coup at the expense of Libya. Appearing on NBC's "Today" program on April 4, the morning of the blast, Burt said the United States had "clear indications" of Libyan involvement. Five days later, following a speech in Atlanta, NATO's supreme commander, General Bernard W. Rogers, said the evidence was beyond dispute. He added that the U.S. government had advance knowledge of a possible attack in West Berlin but that efforts to alert the local nightclubs frequented by American servicemen came "about 15 minutes too late" to save the off-duty troops at La Belle.

Although various officials made no secret of their pride in having penetrated the Libyan signals traffic, the National Security Agency (which records and decodes foreign communications) was alarmed by the statements of General Rogers and Ambassador Burt. It warned recipients who had made public the contents of these highly secret intercepts that they were severely hampering NSA's ability to go on intercepting Libyan communications. Once alerted to the fact that their messages were being intercepted, the Libyans could be expected to change their codes and transmission methods.

The NSA's desire to keep the intercepts secret conflicted, however, with a determination in the White House to rally allied support for a common effort against Libyan terrorism by making them public. The State Department ended up circulating paraphrased versions of the purported Libyan messages to allied capitals, which may have been why several European governments declined to join the United States in applying tough new sanctions. Only the British government saw the raw transcripts and, as mentioned earlier, authorized American F-111 jets based in England to be used in the April 15 air strike against Libyan targets.

Casey Warns the *Post*

The law, beyond question, was on the side of the NSA. Section 798 of United States Code, Title 18, makes it a crime for anyone to transmit—knowingly and willfully—to an unauthorized person, or to publish "any classified information" concerning communications intelligence activities, or "any classified information. . .obtained by the process of communications intelligence from the communications of foreign governments."

CIA director William J. Casey cited that statute less than a month after the Libyan intercept disclosures when he warned *The Washington Post* against publishing what it knew about the NSA project code-named Ivy Bells. The *Post*'s executive editor, Benjamin C. Bradlee, had first heard something about that operation in September 1985, when Bob Woodward came into his office, shut the door, "and in almost a whisper laid out an amazing top secret American intelligence capability that emerged in bits and pieces eight months later in the trial of Ronald Pelton. Woodward described in great detail how the communication intercept had worked, where the communications were intercepted, every detail except Pelton's name. Woodward didn't have Pelton's name because no American knew for sure at that point that a man named Pelton had sold this intelligence gold mine to the Russians five years earlier."

According to Bradlee, the *Post* gave no thought to publishing any of Woodward's information until after Pelton's arrest on November 24. On December 5, at the suggestion of Poindexter, Bradlee and Leonard Downie, the *Post*'s managing editor, talked with Lt. Gen. William Odom, the NSA head. They told Odom about the information they had developed and asked why it should be kept secret in view of the fact that the Soviets had bought the same information from Pelton years before his arrest.

General Odom said, according to Bradlee, that the information was still extremely sensitive, that Washington did not know exactly what the Russians had learned from Pelton, and that any story about the case would gravely threaten the national security. Over the next five months the *Post* worked and reworked the story. "We were determined not to violate the legitimate security of the nation," Bradlee said, "but we were equally determined not to be browbeaten by the administration, which has from time to time appeared to relish press-bashing, into not publishing something that our enemies already knew."

Post editors met Odom at least three times, Bradlee recalled; they talked at least four times with Casey, once with Admiral Poindexter, and once with William Webster, then head of the FBI. At each meeting, different versions of the Pelton story were discussed, and each time the officials invoked national security. The story kept being postponed.

On May 2, Casey suggested a meeting with Bradlee and Downie at the University Club. Casey read the latest version through, tossed it aside and said, "There's no way you can run that story without endangering the national security." He did not mean to threaten anyone, Casey added, but he would have to consider recommending prosecution by the Justice Department if the story was published. "We've already got five absolutely cold violations" of 18 USC 798 against the *Post* and four other news organizations, Casey said. Nine days later, President Reagan called Katharine Graham, chairman of the Washington Post Company, to reinforce Casey's warning. Again the *Post* withheld publication and started to prepare a new version that deleted all the "wiring diagram" details about Ivy Bells.

The *Post* was still sitting on its story when James Polk of NBC News broadcast his own abbreviated version on May 19, 1986. According to the transcript of that morning's "Today" program, Polk reported that "Pelton apparently gave away one of the NSA's most sensitive secrets, a project with the code name Ivy Bells, believed to be a top-secret eavesdropping program by American submarines inside Soviet harbors." Casey responded the same day with a public statement again threatening prosecution: "We believe that the assertions, if true, made by James Polk on the NBC Today show, violate the prohibitions in 18 USC 798 against publishing any classified information concerning the communications intelligence activities of the United States. My statutory obligation to protect intelligence sources and methods requires me to refer this matter to the Department of Justice." Not until the night of May 27 did the *Post* notify the White House, by way of a courtesy to President Reagan, that it would run the much-revised story the next day. It was printed under the bylines of Bob Woodward and Patrick Tyler.[2]

Pelton was convicted on June 6 after seven days of testimony in open court had laid bare details not contained in the original *Post* article.

Although the statute Casey mentioned had been on the books since 1950, it had never led to the prosecution of a news organization. Justice Department officials, in spite of Casey's pressure, apparently declined to prosecute the *Post* or NBC News. George Lauder, a CIA spokesman, acknowledged that "the *Post* did remove some material that was considered damaging." Reminded that the Justice Department seemed less than eager to prosecute, he replied: "We don't run the Justice Department. If people who are sworn to enforce the law decide not to enforce it, that's their business."

The Secret Under Another Name

In fact, stories about eavesdropping operations by U.S. submarines had been published earlier by both the *Post* and *The New York Times,* although those stories did not use the Ivy Bells code name. The *Post* had reported as early as January 4, 1974, in a front-page article by Laurence Sterne, that "the United States maintains a fleet of electronic eavesdropping submarines operating close to the Soviet coastline to monitor Russian submarine activity and secret military communications." The code name used in the Sterne article was Holystone.

Holystone was mentioned again in a series of articles in *The New York Times* by Seymour Hersh, beginning on May 25, 1975. Hersh wrote that the nuclear-powered submarines "were able to plug into Soviet land communication cables strewn across the ocean bottom and thus were able to intercept high-level military messages and other communications considered too important to be sent by radio or other less secure means." The Hersh articles alarmed James R. Schlesinger, who had been director of Central Intelligence from 1973 to 1975 and later became secretary of defense. Schlesinger pressed for prosecution, but the Ford White House preferred not to tangle with the press at that sensitive moment. "It was an altogether different climate at the time in which the idea of prosecuting a reporter was just impossible," Schlesinger later recalled. "You had the CIA's alleged involvement in Watergate. The CIA's reputation on Capitol Hill was mixed and the people in the White House just didn't want to get President Ford involved in prosecution of a reporter."[3]

The threat of prosecution against *The Washington Post,* NBC News, and three other news organizations eleven years later did not, however, deter *The Boston Globe* from publishing additional details about Ivy Bells on June 5, 1986. The *Globe* said its fresh details had been alluded to by Pelton during his espionage trial. All the information, the *Globe* said, had been "previously in the public domain." It claimed, nevertheless, to have omitted some technical details and described others only in general terms under an agreement with "senior U.S. intelligence officials." The most intriguing new detail, according to the *Globe* report, was that thanks to a high-technology device identified by Pelton as a "recording system," the intercepted Soviet messages could be relayed back to the United States by satellite without requiring the eavesdropping submarines to remain in the area—and thus risk capture or destruction.

Press-government tensions eased somewhat after three weeks, with both sides claiming victory. Editors who had published articles about the stolen secrets insisted they had given up nothing in their confrontation with Casey, even though the *Post* had deleted material from the version it finally printed. Bradlee continued to insist the paper had not done "anything different from our normal practice." A CIA spokeswoman, on the other hand, claimed: "A lot of people have paid attention to what we said, and we're pleased about that."

Tracking the Leakers

It remained to be seen whether, or how long, the news organizations would continue to bear in mind that the Communications Intelligence statute was still on the books. The government, in any event, shelved the idea of criminal prosecutions against news organizations. It shifted attention to hunting down federal officials who had leaked classified information, rather than the reporters who published it, though it offered no assurances for the future. Patrick J. Buchanan, an editorial writer and syndicated newspaper columnist before he served as communications director at the White House, observed: "Leaks are like prostitution and gambling. You can control them and contain them a bit—but you're not going to eliminate them."

Even some of Casey's critics within the administration conceded that he had reason to be concerned about the Ivy Bells disclosures. It was always possible, they hinted, that Pelton had not in fact supplied the Soviet Union with all the technical information about that top-secret project. Others, notably Senator Dave Durenberger, the Minnesota Republican who headed the Senate Intelligence Committee, made the point that an administration known to have used intelligence data rather loosely to score political points might not have been in a strong position to press charges:

> They don't think about leaks in terms of Ronald Reagan's declassifying information about terrorist camps in Nicaragua for television purposes. . .or Ronald Reagan believing he needs to sell the American people on bombing Tripoli and Benghazi. That all has serious implications for the collection of communications intelligence. I would start my definition of leaks there.[4]

6 / News, Washington Style

To discuss the leaking of information as if it were a rational and necessary system of communication among Washington players is to assume that the players to whom messages are supposedly being sent via the media understand the senders' intentions. . . . Sometimes things do work this way. But more often the senders are so clever or so inept as to be totally misunderstood, or else the message gets garbled in transmission. . . .The game, however, does give pleasure to the players.

—*Stephen Hess,* The Government/Press Connection

The bulk of the Washington news that Americans read in their newspapers or watch on the television tube does not involve leaks from anonymous sources. In a 1973 study of coverage by *The Washington Post* and *The New York Times,* Leon Sigal found that more than 58 percent came from news conferences, press releases issued by federal agencies, and official proceedings such as congressional hearings. Reporters and scholars disagree, however, about the degree of candor that official spokesmen bring to public sessions, which are open to all comers. Lewis Wolfson of American University in Washington has written: "Officials inevitably put the best face on policy and on the work of their bosses. Successes are promoted and failures downplayed. The official line is not necessarily government's true position on an issue."[1] But Stephen Hess, in a study of information distributed by five federal agencies, argues that their output is neither controversial nor "especially self-serving."

The news of greatest interest to Washington reporters, the stuff that starts their competitive juices flowing, carries a whiff of mystery and the mark of exclusivity. At its least exalted level, this is information that comes out of background briefings, known in the trade as "backgrounders." A medium- to upper-level official, meeting reporters one-

55

on-one or in a select group, will as a rule speak more freely than he would in a large news conference that is open to all. The rule here is non-attribution. The information he provides must, by the rules of the game, be attributed to nameless, faceless persons. "Administration officials," "well-informed sources," and increasingly, just plain "sources" are among the devices reporters use to conceal the actual identity of the source.

No Attribution, Please

As Tom Wicker has written, the rule against direct attribution tends to make a policy explanation at a background session look less partisan, more truly objective, than it is. Bill Moyers, once press secretary to President Lyndon Johnson, has said that the backgrounder "permits the press and government to sleep together, even to procreate, without getting married or having to accept responsibility for any offspring. It's the public on whose doorstep orphans of deceptive information are left, while the press and government roll their eyes innocently and exclaim 'non mea culpa.'"

In short, the traffic in unattributed information, whether through backgrounders or leaks, often carries a tinge of hypocrisy. And because the information is obtained surreptitiously, as Wolfson points out, it may seem far more momentous than it really is. Many leaks in fact have little impact on policy and contribute even less to public understanding of the issues at stake. The definitions in common use tend to be slippery. One reason is that as new officials come to town they bring their own definitions with them.

Dean Rusk, for example, inaugurated a new category of anonymous communication when he coined the term "deep background"—as distinct from just plain background. Rusk presumably knew what he meant by that term, but the reporters who attended his Friday afternoon sessions at the State Department sometimes found the distinction puzzling. Their understanding was that Rusk had no objection to his thoughts masquerading in the newspapers the next day as their own. They had long since become accustomed to practicing this form of compulsory plagiarism. What evidently counted with Rusk was that his remarks not be identified as coming from the State Department. In view of the fact that his audience consisted solely of correspondents prominently identified with the State Department, Rusk's device cannot have provided much cover for the secretary, or his department.

A Game Inside the Beltway

These arcane distinctions may make perfect sense to the small fraction of Americans who live and work "inside the Beltway" that girdles Washington and its close-in suburbs or, more precisely, to the miniscule number of them who are professionally concerned with foreign policy and national security matters. But for the mass of Americans—readers, viewers, voters—they are no more than gibberish. The public, in whose name journalists exercise their First Amendment rights, tends to be only an incidental target of the traffic in leaks and other under-the-counter transactions between government and press. The reader's distance from Washington appears to bear an inverse relationship to his or her interest in these matters.

The Washington Post often has the inside track on secret information for a number of reasons, mainly its intelligent, aggressive staff of reporters and editors. But its edge over *The New York Times* or the *Los Angeles Times* owes something to the fact that the *Post* is the hometown paper for the people who live inside the Beltway, whether they are government employees, lawyers, lobbyists, or journalists. It is the first (in many cases the only) paper they read, the one that covers government as closely as Detroit papers cover the automobile industry.

Both *The New York Times* and the *Los Angeles Times* have appreciably larger circulations than the *Post.* Each maintains a large bureau in Washington, staffed by first-rate journalists. Because neither of the *Times* newspapers is greatly troubled by editorial competition on its home ground, both have targeted the *Post* as their chief competitor in reporting national and international news. The result is a three-cornered struggle to be first. "The competitive juices flow alright," said Craig Whitney, chief of *The New York Times*'s Washington bureau. "The *Post,* after all, is the local paper here. The Beltway pretty much defines its readership. How appropriate is it for the *Times,* with its larger, more national, audience to compete against the *Post?*" Whitney left the question unanswered. It would be very difficult, he conceded, to restrain his "young tigers" from trying to match the *Post,* scoop for scoop and leak for leak.

The three elite newspapers may set the pace, but there are other competitors. *The Wall Street Journal,* for example, is a national paper with its own strong Washington bureau. There are also the three commercial television networks, which increasingly in recent years have come up with their own fresh disclosures out of the Washington bureaucracy. Finally, there are the news magazines—*Time, Newsweek,* and *U.S. News and World Report*—which reach millions of readers every week.

Each of these major media outlets has the attention of the government. Twenty years ago, the TV networks were at a certain disadvantage that tended to reduce the impact of their reporting out of Washington. Most senior officials were not in the habit of watching the evening news programs on television. They were still at work in the early evening hours. But, as John Chancellor points out, the times and technology have changed. "Nowadays," he said, "I am read, though still not seen, by those high officials." An internal government publication called *Current News,* published daily by the air force for the Defense Department, reprints or summarizes the news and commentary broadcast by the networks.

Inner Ring, Outer Ring

The pecking order among reporters and the news organizations they serve has its counterpart in the government itself. Thomas E. Cronin has diagramed the relationship between an inner ring of government departments (the White House, State, Treasury, and Justice) and all the rest, which he consigned to the outer ring.[2] So it is with news organizations, according to Hess. In his diagram, the inner ring consists of eleven media organizations: *The Washington Post, The New York Times,* and *The Wall Street Journal*; two news agencies, Associated Press and United Press International; the three news magazines and three television networks. Hess's middle ring includes large independent newspapers such as the *Chicago Tribune,* large newspaper chains like Gannett (and presumably also Knight-Ridder), and the Cable News Network. All the rest, it must be assumed, have been banished to the outer ring, which means less preferred treatment.[3] In short, the power and prestige of the news organization, rather than the individual reporter's energy and intelligence, determine his or her treatment.

It is an intricate diagram, erring perhaps in the attempt to find a slot somewhere for everyone, as in India's traditional caste system. Judging by the author's Washington experience over a fifteen-year period, it is also too neatly mechanical. There is no reason to doubt that a hierarchical organization like the federal government will be quicker to return a call from *The New York Times* than from Cleveland's *Plain Dealer.* Hess discounts, however, the fact that particular reporters have risen above the predetermined status of their newspapers by reason of their uncommon ability, range of contacts, and length of service.

The *Baltimore Sun,* a case in point, would probably fit into the middle ring constructed by Hess. Its legendary Pentagon correspondent, Mark Watson, suffered no visible disadvantage although he did not represent an inner-ring organization. He was, in his day, the most admired and respected of the lot. Charles Corddry, one of Watson's successors, enjoys similar standing today. Personal merit, reinforced by long acquaintance, can overcome the tendency of some officials to favor high-status organizations.

As the national audience has grown, so has the size and visibility of the Washington press corps, thanks in large part to a more than fourfold increase of radio and television reporters assigned to Washington over the past two decades. There are now approximately 10,000 journalists representing more than 3,000 news organizations operating out of Washington. The public's access to information about government has increased commensurately. An eloquent measure of the distance we have come is provided by William L. Rivers:

> Thirty years ago, when D. W. Brogan wrote his classic *Politics in America,* he did not consider it necessary even to mention the role of the media in the American political process. Today, after Vietnam and particularly after Watergate, a political analyst, such as Paul Weaver, will insist...that the reliance of television news on the "single omniscient observer, and its commitment to the notion of a unified thematic depiction of events—all make TV an extraordinarily powerful mobilizer of public attention and public opinion....Television news . . . is perhaps the most powerful centralizing machine ever let loose in American society."[4]

The New Role of the Press

Present-day media serve two major democratic functions: They are the citizen's main source of information about what is happening in government; they also have become an important mechanism, though not the only one, that informs government about the state of public feelings and attitudes. Both functions used to be performed by political parties through their leaders. "The media in the United States are the new political parties," James David Barber has written. "The old political parties are gone. What we now have are television and print."[5] It is a provocative suggestion.

7 / The Price of Secrecy

The fruits of U.S. secrecy are having an unhealthy effect. . . .Nuclear weapons have been developed under a maximum amount of secrecy. The Soviet Union is probably ahead of the U.S. Practically no governmental secrecy, only mild proprietary limitations, have been introduced in the development of computers. The U.S. is undoubtedly ahead of the Soviets in this field. Secrecy does not lead to security.

—Edward Teller

Many reporters have been slow to recognize that their common practice of granting anonymity to leakers puts them on slippery moral ground. They allow themselves to be used, many thoughtful reporters concede, for purposes they do not always comprehend. When they stand behind their nameless sources, they are vouching for the truthfulness of those sources, frequently (though not in every case) without more than perfunctory checking. "The leaker always has some self-serving motive, good or bad, but gets off scot-free while accomplishing his purpose," as Thomas Griffith has written. The citizen, seldom schooled in the jargon or folkways of Washington, may well feel shortchanged when he reads or hears that "a high official" or "a source," whose bias or special interest has not been divulged, has made a disclosure about arms-control policy or the progress of SDI. Griffith's remedy is more candor: "Without betraying its anonymous sources (who often bring to light what needs to be known), the press needs to do a better job of suggesting in the story itself just what interests and motivations are involved in its publication."[1]

Vice President Bush, on the other hand, has been less critical of the media than of those officials who do the leaking. In a 1981 interview, the vice president said: "I really feel we have been undisciplined in this White House. We've not served the President well by the leaks. I know the people writing the stories, and I have confidence in the integrity of many of them. So when certain reporters say they've got a high White House source or a State Department source or a Defense Department source, I'm convinced they've got a source. That means somebody has behaved very badly and in an immature way."[2]

A leak is the outcome of a transaction between reporter and source, and, like other successful transactions, it necessarily serves the interests of both parties. As long as those mutual interests are served, it seems unlikely that leaks will vanish from the Washington scene in the foreseeable future. A survey of former federal officials in policymaking positions, conducted by the Institute of Politics at Harvard's Kennedy School of Government, found that no fewer than 42 percent of those questioned acknowledged that they had leaked while in office. Nearly four out of five said they leaked to counter false or misleading information. Almost as many, three out of four, said they leaked to gain attention for a policy option or issue. Then, in descending order, 64 percent said they leaked to consolidate support from the public or a constituency outside of government; 53 percent, to force action on an issue; 32 percent, to send a message to another part of the government; 31.5 percent, to stop action on an issue; 30 percent, to test reactions to a policy consideration; 30 percent, to protect their own position; 29 percent, in response to an enterprising reporter's skill and persistence in eliciting information.[3]

Stuart Eizenstat, who was in charge of domestic policy for President Carter, was one of the few former officials interviewed who said he believed in the efficacy of leaks. Eizenstat favored the "conscious planned leak," adding that the Carter administration could have used leaks more than it did to test congressional and public reactions to presidential decisions under consideration. Brzezinski, who served the same president, continues to insist that he did no leaking. "Someone at my level never leaks," he said.[4] As indicated earlier, Brzezinski exonerated himself by redefining the word. Former Secretary of State Cyrus Vance, often the target of Brzezinski's disclosures, said that leaking was "one of the most corrosive practices that goes on in Washington."

No End in Sight

For all the criticism of leaks and leakers, neither the press nor the upper bureaucracy has changed its ways. A leak-free Washington seems as remote today as the fulfillment of Isaiah's prophecy about a world of just men beating swords into plowshares. Several reasons come to mind:

- Too much secrecy, often misapplied to information that is trivial, or of slight importance, by officials who wield the "top secret" stamp more or less indiscriminately. The Defense Department alone is estimated to have 1,500,000 top-secret documents locked in its safes. From 1973 to 1984, the number of documents classified by the government jumped 60 percent, according to the staff study on *The Protection of National Secrets*. Knowledgeable Republicans and Democrats in Congress tend to agree that the obsession with secrecy leads many officials to overclassify information of no great significance to national security. One perverse effect of this obsession has been to debase the classification system and to endow inherently trivial information with a spurious importance in the eyes of leak-happy reporters. Another more serious result, according to the physicist Edward Teller, is that highly qualified scientists are barred from discussions of defense problems for lack of the required clearance.
- Too many officials cleared to handle top-secret information. When four million federal officials (most of them assigned to routine low-level tasks) are cleared for access to classified information, it is hard for them to take the system seriously. They have seen bureaucrats in the middle and upper reaches of the federal establishment ignore security classifications when it served their political advantage to do so. Leaks designed to sway congressional votes on defense spending, covert operations, changes in tax law, and other less sensitive issues have become an accepted *modus operandi* for both parties, undermining respect for the system among those who operate it.
- The continued prevalence of internal government tensions and disputes over policy matters, providing individuals or factions with an incentive to leak in order to advance their goals, or to counter the goals of others. As we have seen, the issue may be arms for Afghan resistance fighters or early deployment of the Strategic Defense Initiative, or it may reflect a power struggle as in the campaigns to oust

Secretary of State Haig or National Security Adviser Richard Allen. In each case, the Washington press corps played a central role by disseminating leaks from one side or the other, or both. The press did not invent the inner tensions that produced these leaks. But, because it cannot resist a "good story," it served the interests and designs of the leakers, in most cases without identifying those interests for the public.

- The diminishing number of editors who press their reporters to name and evaluate the sources of a story before they agree to publish it. This widespread reluctance to challenge the sources of high-flying investigative reporters raises serious questions about press responsibility. It is a recent phenomenon, dating from the Watergate/Vietnam period, with its emphasis on tough-minded, deep-digging adversarial journalism. A less fortunate by-product was the spread of a "trust me" mentality among certain reporters, who resisted naming their sources even in confidential discussions with their editors. Bob Woodward, for example, recalls that he froze when Katharine Graham, publisher of *The Washington Post* at the time of its Watergate investigation, asked him to tell *her* the name of Deep Throat. He would have given her the name if she insisted, Woodward wrote, but he was praying she would not press the matter. Graham did not insist. She laughed and said she was kidding.[5] It is not, however, a laughing matter when the responsible head of a major newspaper hesitates to ask a reporter a truth-seeking question of this sort.

- The reward system in American journalism. A reporter profits by appearing to be more enterprising and better-informed than his colleagues or competitors. That way lies professional recognition, salary increases, and the path to advancement. It hardly seems coincidental that each of the last three executive editors of *The New York Times*—James Reston, A. M. Rosenthal, and Max Frankel—made his reputation as a first-class reporter before reaching the top. All three have won Pulitzer Prizes and countless lesser honors. Bradlee of the *Post* is another example, although he did his best reporting for *Newsweek* before taking command of the *Post*.

The Costs of Leaking

Although leaks seem to be here to stay, they have their costs. Perhaps the most compelling argument against the practice, an argument made by Hess and other critics, is that leaks, or the fear of leaks, may distort the policymaking process:

> Especially in situations in which presidents have a strong desire to maintain surprise, the lesson they seem to learn in order to avoid leaks is to turn inward: involve the minimum number of advisers in the formulation stage and compartmentalize so that technicians will not know how the pieces are going to be fitted together. The problem, of course, as Jody Powell pointed out, is that "the damage done by leaks must be carefully balanced against the damage done by excluding people who can contribute to the decision-making process."[6]

Although Hess published his study two years before Ronald Reagan stubbed his toe on the Iran-contra affair, his analysis neatly fits the circumstances of that abortive enterprise. The secretaries of state and defense were excluded from the latter stages of planning because they disapproved of the radical policy change it represented. That left CIA Director Casey as the sole cabinet-level official with unchallenged authority to advise and direct the operations of Colonel North—at considerable cost to the president's reputation.

Richard Nixon made much the same mistake when he shut himself off from senior administration officers who might have warned him, in advance of the Watergate crisis, that the covert course he had chosen could have disastrous consequences for his presidency. Fear that the truth may out, in short, has been a poor guide for presidential action in recent years.

Leaks have a short life span. They fade from public memory as soon as their novelty wears off. How many Americans today retain even a vague recollection of the Pentagon Papers, leaked to the press by Daniel Ellsberg in 1971? Yet it's worth recalling that President Nixon's decision to set up the so-called Plumbers unit, a direct response to the Ellsberg leak, led inexorably to the Watergate break-in and to his eventual resignation when faced with impeachment. Most leaks, of course, deal with far less momentous issues.

The Road to Improvement

It is difficult to conceive of a constitutional remedy that would end the practice of leaking without doing violence to the fabric of American freedoms. There is room, however, for voluntary reforms. For example, a decent skepticism about the motives of leakers on the part of the media would help. The leaker's interest or bias should be identified, even when he cannot be named. Readers and television audiences, as Jody Powell has written, "have a right to know something about the possible prejudices of its sources....If a reporter's source has a clear and identifiable stake in the outcome of the issue under discussion, the reader ought to be told, but usually is not. Comments from 'informed sources' on the tar baby incident would be infinitely more informing to the reader if it were known whether they came from an associate of Brer Rabbit or Brer Fox."[7]

There are relatively few examples, unfortunately, of reporters who have taken the trouble to identify the source's bias in this fashion. One notable exception was a story by Robert Pear in *The New York Times,* on April 25, 1987, that ran under the headline:

"DUARTE APPEALS TO REAGAN TO LET SALVADORANS STAY"

The Salvadoran president, Jose Napoleon Duarte, had sent a confidential letter to Mr. Reagan expressing alarm over the effects of the new U.S. immigration law on "some 400,000 to 600,000 Salvadorans" who had entered the country illegally since 1982 and would, therefore, not qualify for amnesty under the terms of the new legislation. Duarte requested temporary refuge for them, contending that their deportation would be disastrous to the Salvadoran economy. Pear dealt with the attribution problem in a single short paragraph: "A copy of Mr. Duarte's letter was obtained by *The New York Times* from a person sympathetic to his request and to the plight of Salvadorans in the United States." That one sentence told the reader all he needed to know about the motives of the person who leaked the letter to the *Times.* It may be difficult, though surely not impossible, for more reporters in and out of Washington to play fair with their readers in this way. The effort would be justified over time by increased public understanding and respect for the job journalists do.

In addition, editors and publishers could help by overcoming their reluctance to ask their reporters hard questions about sources. When high officials of the Nixon administration, including the attorney general and the White House counsel, were threatening *The Washington Post* with retribution for its Watergate coverage, Graham and her editors had powerful reasons to question reporters about their sources. Apparently they did not press the matter with Woodward and Bernstein, which may have done wonders for the morale of that intrepid pair. But the relationship between reporter and editor must be based on *mutual* trust. Reporters who expect to be trusted by their editors ought in turn to show comparable trust in the discretion of those editors.

Leaks have been so plentiful in the Reagan years that the Washington preoccupation with doing something to stop them is understandable. It would be unrealistic, however, to imagine that the traffic is likely to be halted or greatly diminished by new legislation or harsh administrative restrictions. When a so-called secret is revealed by the media, it is important to remember that the secret was created by an official, armed with a rubber stamp, who may have given little thought to its inherent sensitivity or potential for damage to the national security. The fact that a piece of information bears the secret stamp may perversely increase its appeal to a reporter.

One way of cutting down on the traffic in leaks, as the congressional staff study cited earlier suggests, would be for the government to sift through its mountains of documents stamped secret and systematically declassify those that do not warrant protection. Not all secrets, in short, are equal. Another forward step would be to cut back severely the number of officials who are authorized to declassify information on their own authority.

The leaks that matter in Washington are almost always the work of "political players rather than bureaucratic moles," as Hodding Carter has noted. The Reagan administration, like its recent predecessors, has turned a blind eye to leaks authorized by senior officials. It is the unauthorized leaks, mostly by middle-level officials, that worry the White House. Many of these have been traced to officials appointed by President Reagan, and to Republicans in Congress, who share his proclaimed policy goals but contend that he has strayed from the true path.[8]

This is a new phenomenon that bears careful watching. Only two middle-level officials have been fired for what seem to be leaks motivated by right-wing ideology. That may be the administration's only resort so long as true-blue conservatives go on leaking in what they apparently insist is the president's best interest. The more dignified alternative would be to resign on an issue of principle, as Cyrus Vance did over President Carter's decision to attempt the helicopter rescue of the Teheran embassy hostages. But resignations of this sort, while fairly common in Britain, are exceptions in the United States.

How Realistic Is It to Hope for Voluntary Reform?

As for the press, its instinctive rejection of self-improvement schemes as far back as the Hutchins Commission report in 1947 leaves little room for hope of wholesale voluntary reform. At a minimum, editors would do well to consider *The Washington Post* rule, born of nervous uncertainty about some of its Watergate sources, that anonymous information must be verified before publication by at least two independent sources. They might also consider the importance to the reader of identifying the bias of an anonymous source without giving his name, as a few Washington reporters have done from time to time. "Even for the best of reasons," Edward Jay Epstein has written, "if journalists represent news as being accidental when in fact it is deliberate, then they may willy-nilly assist in camouflaging the interest behind the disclosure, and thereby be part on a grander scale of the cover-up of an intra-government power struggle."[9]

Any critical examination of the surreptitious traffic in leaks risks losing sight of the truth in Bruce Catton's statement that "our particular form of government won't work without it."[10] Catton was a Washington reporter and government information officer before he turned to writing Civil War history. Another old Washington hand, the Harvard political scientist Richard E. Neustadt, believes that leaks play "a vital role in the functioning of our democracy."[11]

For all the discomfort they have caused to a succession of presidents, leaks are bound to persist, and the White House will remain their most important source. As one presidential aide told Lou Cannon of *The Washington Post* in 1983, "there is no evidence that reporters were told anything we didn't want them to know."

Notes

Chapter 1

1. From Robert J. McCloskey, "How Not to Stop Leaks," *The Washington Post,* February 1, 1982, reprinted in Stephen Hess, *The Government/Press Connection* (Washington, D.C.: Brookings, 1984).

Chapter 2

1. Letter to Congress, May 5, 1777, in *Writings of George Washington* (Washington, D.C.: Government Printing Office, 1933), vol. VIII, p. 17.

2. *Droit de l'Information,* Paris, 1976.

3. Quoted in Mary A. Best, *Thomas Paine, Prophet and Martyr of Democracy* (New York: Harcourt Brace, 1927), p. 146.

4. Moncure D. Conway, *Life of Thomas Paine* (Norwood, Pennsylvania: Norwood, 1977), p. 38.

5. Robert C. Alberts, *The Golden Voyage: The Life and Times of William Bingham* (Boston: Houghton Mifflin, 1969), p. 19.

6. Larry L. Burriss, "America's First Newspaper Leak: Tom Paine and the Disclosure of Secret French Aid to the United States," Ph.D. diss., Ohio University, 1983. Much of the narrative concerning the Paine-Deane scandal is drawn from that source, with the author's permission.

Chapter 3

1. George E. Reedy, *The Twilight of the Presidency* (Waco, Texas: World, 1970), p. 110.

2. Laurence Barrett, *Gambling With History: Reagan in the White House* (New York: Doubleday, 1983), p. 430.

3. Seymour Hersh, *The Price of Power: Kissinger in the Nixon White House* (New York: Summit Books, 1983), pp. 470-71.

4. William Greider, "Reporters and Their Sources," *The Washington Monthly,* October 1982, p. 14. The article was adapted from Greider's

book, *The Education of David Stockman and Other Americans* (New York: Dutton, 1982).

5. Hess, *The Government/Press Connection,* pp. 77-78.

6. Martin Linsky, *Impact: How the Press Affects Federal Policymaking* (New York: Norton, 1986), p. 195.

7. For the text of the Weinberger letter, see *The New York Times,* November 16, 1985, p. 7.

8. Dusko Doder, "Michael Pillsbury: The Agonies of Victory in Government's Substratum," *The Washington Post,* January 26, 1987.

9. Jonathan Alter, "When Sources Get Immunity," *Newsweek,* January 19, 1987, p. 54.

10. *SAIS Review,* Winter 1981.

Chapter 4

1. Deposition of Max Frankel in *The United States of America v. The New York Times Company, et al.* District Court of the Southern District of New York, June 17, 1971.

2. Richard Halloran, "A Primer on the Fine Art of Leaking Information," *The New York Times,* January 14, 1983.

3. *Political Communication and Persuasion,* vol. 3, no. 1, pp. 91-92.

4. Ibid, p. 84.

Chapter 5

1. Roland S. Inlow, "An Appraisal of the Morison Espionage Trial," in *First Principles: National Security and Civil Liberties,* vol. 11, no. 4, pp. 1-5.

2. Benjamin C. Bradlee, "The *Post* and Pelton: How the Press Looks at National Security," *The Washington Post,* June 8, 1986, p. F-1.

3. Stephen Engelberg, "U.S. Aides Said to Have Discussed Prosecuting News Organizations," *The New York Times,* May 21, 1986.

4. Doyle McManus, "Cordial Truce Over Leaks Foreshadows Battles Yet to Come," *Los Angeles Times,* June 9, 1986, p. 6.

Chapter 6

1. Lewis W. Wolfson, *The Untapped Power of the Press* (New York: Praeger, 1985), p. 84.

2. Thomas E. Cronin, *The State of the Presidency* (Boston: Little Brown, 1975), pp. 188-92.

3. Hess, *The Government/Press Connection,* p. 101.

4. William L. Rivers, *The Other Government: Power & the Washington Media* (New York: Universe Books, 1982), p. 172.

5. James David Barber, a personal communication, cited in Linsky, *Impact,* p. 10.

Chapter 7

1. Thomas Griffith, "A Sinking Feeling About Leaks," *Time,* December 22, 1980, p. 81.

2. *U.S. News and World Report,* December 14, 1981, p. 20.

3. Linsky, *Impact,* pp. 196-97.

4. Ibid., p. 201.

5. Carl Bernstein and Bob Woodward, *All the President's Men* (New York: Warner Books, 1975), pp. 262-63.

6. Hess, *The Government/Press Connection,* pp. 93-94.

7. Jody Powell, *The Other Side of the Story* (New York: William Morrow and Company, 1984), p. 17.

8. Hodding Carter III, "Firing Guilty Officials is the Way to Plug Leaks," *The Wall Street Journal,* May 22, 1986, p. 31.

9. Edward Jay Epstein, "The Grand Cover-Up," *The Wall Street Journal,* April 19, 1976.

10. Quoted in Douglas Cater, *The Fourth Branch of Government* (New York: Vintage, 1959), p. 137.

11. Quoted by William Safire, *Safire's Political Dictionary* (New York: Ballantine, 1980), p. 369.

Index

DATE DUE

NOV 4 '99			
NOV 3 '01			
MAY 0 0 2006			

WITHDRAWN

DEMCO 38-297